How to Meet Your SPIRIT GUIDES, ANGELS and POWER ANIMALS

Spiritual Guidance On Demand in 5 to 10 Minutes

A Practical Guide

Tianna Galgano

© 2012 by Tianna Galgano

ISBN-13: 978-1479170937
ISBN-10: 1479170933

All Rights Reserved. No part of this publication may be reproduced in any form or by any means, including scanning, photocopying, or otherwise without prior written permission of the copyright holder.

First Printing, 2012

Printed in the United States of America

Liability Disclaimer

By reading this book, you assume all risks associated with using the advice given herein, with a full understanding that you, solely, are responsible for anything that may occur as a result of putting this information into action in any way, and regardless of your interpretation of the advice.

The suggestions and meditations in this practical guide are not intended to take the place of medical advice, or clinical therapy. You are encouraged to seek out a qualified, certified professional if you have suffered a trauma; or have depression, PTSD, inner child issues, anxiety, or any other emotional/mental condition. See your physician for tests and diagnosis before doing a meditation for healing any physical condition you may have. You can certainly use the healing meditation(s) as a companion to a doctor's advice and recommendations. The author holds no responsibility for negative results from doing any of the meditations suggested whether you are following the steps in this book, or listening to them on the companion recordings.

Terms of Use

You are given a non-transferable, "personal use" license to this book. You cannot distribute it or share it with other individuals.
Also, there are no resale rights or private label rights granted when purchasing this book. In other words, it's for your own personal use only.

Copyright Notice

All meditations and exercises in this Practical Guide and the companion meditation recordings are not to be given out and/or sold as copied reproductions. They may not be reproduced in your own articles and/or books, classes, blogs or websites without prior written permission from the author. Written permission can and in most cases will be granted if Tianna Galgano is credited as the author of this material and as the originator of the exercises and meditations herein.
If you do wish to use material from this book please contact the author at: Tianna@DreamDecipher.com

How to Meet Your SPIRIT GUIDES, ANGELS and POWER ANIMALS

Spiritual Guidance On Demand in 5 to 10 Minutes

A Practical Guide

Tianna Galgano

"The spirit won't stand waiting for years
until the mechanics of learning are mastered.

It must be enlisted from the first
or it will fly away to other things."

Robert Frost

Table of Contents

Introduction 8

Chapter 1: **What Is a Spirit Guide?** 10

Chapter 2: **Why Would You Need a Spirit Guide?**
What can guides do for you? 16
    Meditation: *Meet an Important Spirit Guide* 23

Chapter 3: **Angels and Saints** 25
    Meditation: *Meet Your Guardian Angel* 26

Chapter 4: **Wise Beings** 28

Chapter 5: **Higher Self** 30
    Meditation: *Meet Your Higher Self* 39

Chapter 6: **Animal Guides - Power Animal** 40
    Meditation: *Meet a Power Animal* 48

Chapter 7: **Deceased Loved Ones** 49
    Includes Dream Program:
    Ask for a dearly departed loved one to visit you 57

Chapter 8: **Spirit Guides in Dreams** 58

Chapter 9: **Perceiving Your Guides** 63

Chapter 10: **The Science of Perception** 66
    Visual Imagery Exercise – How You See 71

Chapter 11: **Intuition** 73
    Recognizing How You Perceive Intuitions
    Exercise: *Intuition Location-Finder* 76

Chapter 12: **Overcoming Your Fears**........................83
        Exercise: *Releasing Fear*........................86

Chapter 13: **What You Need to Know
              Before Doing a Meditation**........................89

Chapter 14: **Preparation for Meditation**........................97

Chapter 15: **Meditations - Meet Specific Spirit Guides**........100

   1. *Meet An Important Guide*........................102
   2. *Call on a Spirit Guide for Particular Need/Project*........107
   3. *Meet Your Guardian Angel*........................109
   4. *Meet Your Power Animal – Part One*........................110
   5. *Power Animal, Part Two:
      Merge With Your Power Animal*........................111
   6. *Meet Your Higher Self*........................113
   7. *Meet a Money Guide - Part One*........................115
   8. *Money Guide, Part Two:
      Transform blocks & limiting beliefs about money*........116
   9. *Ask For a Healing Guide*........................119
   10. *Meet With Your Successful Future Self*........................122
   11. *Visit With a Deceased Loved One*........................125

Author's Biography........................127

RESOURCES........................128-129

Introduction

Experience profound ways to **achieve spiritual mastery** in just five to ten minutes a day—whether you are a beginner or have been meditating for awhile.

This Practical Guide has fourteen meditations designed to have you meet numerous types of spirit guides, including angels and power animals. It teaches practical methods for interacting with guides and how to experience spiritual inner journeys with them. There are suggestions for good questions to ask of the guides that provide quality answers and insightful information.

By practicing each meditation several times, it will become effortless to call on any guide "on demand." A guide will appear instantly when spiritual help is wanted or needed.

Besides learning brand new ways to communicate with spirit guides, angels and power animals already in one's awareness, meditations include ways to call upon guides for any project or goal, such as writing, healing, learning a new skill, and so on.

Discover new spirit guides: The meditations encourage guides to appear that one may never have thought about before, such as meeting with Higher Self, a money guide, and a healing guide. A bonus meditation: "Merge With a Power Animal" is a profound way to obtain an animal's power through the body's kinesthetic (*feeling*) system. One can then travel with the power animal as if seeing through its eyes.

Some of the meditations include shamanic methods of healing, such as soul rescue (soul retrieval), which helps one travel into the subconscious, find a past traumatic memory and then rescue the younger self trapped within it.

For those working on self-growth, abundance, creativity and/or healing, a unique meditation asks a spirit guide to lead them directly to a future self who has already become what they desire to be, or who has already achieved a goal. The future self will communicate and provide the steps necessary to achieve this goal. The future self teaches the present self how to become this new self. This meditation includes merging with the future self to achieve the feeling of mastery.

Children benefit from *How to Meet your Spirit Guides*. Numerous stories are included of how children used the meditations to communicate with their guides, angels and power animals. They had profound, amazing results. Children were able to get answers to troubling questions and even to heal themselves. This book enables parents and grandparents to teach their children and grandchildren simple, effective ways to tune into Spirit. The short meditations work well for children as young as four or five. Many of the longer meditations work great for pre-teens and teens.

Intuition Development: Several chapters include in-depth intuition training. Intuition is the primary tool for deciphering symbols and metaphors, whether experienced within a meditation or a dream. An exercise helps the readers discover their intuitive voice, intuitive vision and intuitive feelings in a way they never knew was possible. From then on, a simple, directed eye-movement is all it takes to access one's Voice of Intuition, which allows spiritual guidance on demand, in just a few minutes.

Chapter 1

WHAT IS A SPIRIT GUIDE?

My first experiences with spirit guides

Back in 1983, I had two dreams that impacted me so greatly that to this day I have never forgotten them. In the first dream I was shown that I gave my mom the ability to drive a car again. I thought this was impossible. Mom had not driven in twenty years because she had extreme numbness in her legs and feet. It made pressing on the brake pedal too difficult for safety.

The very next night my Grandma Carrie appeared to me in a dream. I was astounded by this visit because my Grandma, (who was my mom's mother), had been deceased for twenty years. I had never dreamt of her before.

In this dream, Grandma told me that I **could help my mom drive again**. Grandma had come to me in her spirit form in order to explain my previous dream. She told me that my mom had suffered a trauma as a child. Grandma helped me understand that I would have to put the dream of helping my mom drive on hold until I learned how to heal Mom's emotional trauma. Grandma Carrie coming to me in this dream was my very first experience in getting direct communication from a guide in spirit form.

Grandma's spirit stayed close by for several months. I began to hear her voice in my ear during the day. She suggested that I start taking classes in meditation and spiritual growth. I followed her advice.

These two dreams were so impactful and felt so right. They sparked a curiosity about dreams I'd never had before. I began doing dream research with a passion that to this day is ever-present. I attracted a shaman guide who worked closely with me to help create my "Dream Decipher Interpretation Process."

In those early days I opened my home to two ongoing study groups. One night a week the group worked with their dreams. On a different night we read and discussed the Seth material. Seth was a *highly evolved spirit guide,* channeled by Jane Roberts. The profound information in his book, *The Nature of Personal Reality,* blew me away. Our group discussed Seth's concepts at length. It was heady stuff for a beginner on the spiritual path. Yet, the teachings felt so right.

That same year I searched out other spiritual, metaphysical and holistic-themed books and read over a hundred of them. I also meditated regularly. In working so closely with Spirit, I became a much different person. I felt that most of my life I had been walking around half-asleep. Now I was more consciously aware and able to help others. That felt so fulfilling.

One year later, I was invited to Denver, Colorado to attend a Seth conference. A woman came running up to me and thrust an NLP (Neuro-Linguistic Programming) book into my hands. She said in a firm tone, "You need to take this training." I had never met this woman before. But I *knew* Spirit had sent her to me.

I read the book. Many of the transformational case studies gave me the spirit-chills. I *knew* this was the path I needed to follow to help my mom heal her legs and be able to drive again. Thus began my career as a transformational therapist.

After an intensive Master NLP Certification training program in Boulder, Colorado, I was finally ready to approach my mom with an offer.

"Mom, how would you like to be able to drive again?" I asked.

"But I would have to heal my legs," she replied.

"Yes," I said. "And I believe I have a way to help you do that."

The happy ending to this story is that after several months of NLP sessions, I did help Mom heal the numbness in her legs. Through our sessions she discovered the childhood trauma that had caused her legs to become weak. We were able to successfully transform and heal her inner child. As a result, Mom regained the strength in her legs. She was so excited about being able to drive again that she bought a new car. That blew the entire family away.

Definitions and history of spirit guides

I had discovered for myself how easy it was to meet my guides in meditations. I then found I could intuitively interact with them during my waking day. I'm going to show you how to do this too!

But before we begin to learn how to meet and interact with your guides, I'd like to give you some background about spirit guides throughout time.

The Western tradition definition of the term, **"spirit guide**" is: An entity that remains a disincarnate spirit, in order to act as a guide and protector to a living human being.

In other words, a guide is a spirit that resides on another plane or dimension, does not have a physical body, and is a part of a hierarchy of spiritual helpers for souls on earth. Spirit guides are wise, evolved souls or beings that have specific knowledge that is available to us when we ask for it.

Those with wisdom have known throughout history and across civilizations that spirit helpers are there for you—whether you realize it consciously or not.

Spirit guides are liaisons or messengers between an earth soul and a Higher Power. Depending on a person's religious and/or spiritual beliefs, there are of course many names for the Higher Power. You may call this Divine essence: God, The Almighty, The Creator, Spirit, The Great Spirit, The Source, Source Energy, The Universe, The All That Is, Jehovah, Allah, gods, goddesses, and so on. Many people also pray to Jesus and/or his mother, Mary.

I arbitrarily use the terms Higher Spirit, or Spirit, with the S capitalized. While reading along, please do substitute your own term. It is important to follow your own beliefs when connecting and communicating with Higher guidance.

Spirit guide are not on, or of, the Earthly plane. They are from what some refer to as "the other side" or the realm of Higher Spirit. The spiritual realm has a much less dense atmosphere and a higher vibration than Earth. Therefore in order to tune into our guides, it is beneficial to free the mind of earthly concerns—at least for five to fifteen minutes. The short meditations found in the last chapter will help you do that.

Types of guides

Just as The Higher Power has many names, spirit guides are also known by many different names. What a particular guide is called can depend on the beliefs of different religious and spiritual traditions.

There are many different forms that spirit guides can take. These include Higher Selves, angels, saints, wise beings, light beings, and enlightened ones. It is important to note that animals and other creatures can also be spirit guides. These are known as power animals

Within spiritual churches in the past, spirit guides were often stereotyped ethnically. For example, it was popular to call upon Native Americans,

Chinese, Egyptians or Tibetans as guides because of the ancient wisdom they possessed. These kinds of guides are also known as the ancestors and ancient ones.

In traditional religions, guides are called angels and saints. In other belief systems guides may be called spirit guides, Higher Self, wise beings and power animals.

If you seek a particular type of guide, then it is certainly possible to invite one to you. It always works to your advantage to state your intention before you begin a meditation. Allow the appropriate guide for that intention to choose you. When you meet your guide in meditation, it will identify itself according to its background and the role it plays for you.

Thus far, I have been discussing guides that come from different dimensions other than the earth plane. I have suggested that you can call upon a guide to *come to you* from these other realms.

Some, however, might be uncomfortable with the idea of a spiritual essence or energy outside of themselves. For example, you may have the belief that Spirit is *within* you. It is <u>not</u> necessary to externalize a guide to have quality information come through intuitively. Keep an open mind to the suggestions given in the meditations in the last chapter. Amend them to suit your beliefs. Instead of the guidance coming from an outer source, you can think of it as *inner* guidance. You perhaps could be open to the idea of spirit helpers *within* your body or mind.

Where do spirit guides originate?

Some spirit guides are evolved souls who have lived many former lifetimes, paid their karmic debts and advanced beyond a need to reincarnate. Because they learned a series of lessons over numerous lifetimes, they are wiser and more advanced than souls still going through a reincarnation cycle.

After highly evolved souls no longer need to reincarnate, they can choose to become guides to the human race. They do this out of a sense of service to humanity. These guides usually have a unique skill or talent that they can teach to a person who requests it. These spirits can be called upon to provide ongoing guidance in specific situations. For example, writers can have writing guides. Healers can have healing guides. Teachers can have teaching guides. Artists can have artist guides, and so on.

Some spirit guides are not of human origin. That is, certain guides can be evolved souls who never had an earth life, but gained their wisdom in other dimensions, or other realms of reality. These types of guide have always lived solely as energy in the cosmic realm and are known as *light beings*. They are thought to be very high level guides that reside in the highest dimensions.

Very advanced-level guides can have vast knowledge to impart. Some have an understanding of the complexities of higher math, or quantum physics and how the universe works. Others know the complex nature of the subconscious mind and the psyche. Many are experts on the workings of the human body. They can tell us the hidden causes of pain, illness and disease.

Guides can help us understand all these mysteries and more.

There have been and still are some humans on the earth that have a higher vibration. They are able to tune into or "channel" these very high level guides and bring forth astounding information. One such well-known channel was Edgar Cayce. Another was Jane Roberts, author of the Seth books.

Chapter Two

WHY WOULD YOU NEED A SPIRIT GUIDE?

What can guides do for you?

There are different types of guides for different purposes. As their title indicates, they provide guidance and assistance. They can keep you safe by warning you of danger. Some guides are protectors. Some are teachers and can help you gain knowledge. Some are healers and can help you heal yourself.

If you are studying any form of the healing arts in order to help others, you can ask your guides to teach you. Guides can tap into the ancient healing arts and retrieve knowledge that has been 'lost' to modern culture.

Some guides have a skill or talent that you can tune into and utilize for a project you are working on, such as writing, art, creating music, and so on. Creative guides are also known as *muses*.

As an example, I belong to an authors' group. At every meeting we do a meditation to welcome in our writing guides. We also ask for teams of guides to assist us for success. Upon request, the guides on our team tell us what their roles are. On my writing / success team, for example, a couple of my guides help me write. The rest have jobs that support my writing in some way. One guide focuses on editing, another on publishing and a third one works on marketing ideas.

Guides fill important roles. They can point us in the right direction. They are allies on inner journeys. Their power can be called on for your use. You can utilize your guides for all of the above and more.

How does prayer fit in with the concept of spirit guides?

Many religious people pray to God. In their experience God answers their prayers in different ways. When people pray, however, they don't usually expect God to answer directly. Most don't try to have a conversation with the Higher Power. Usually a prayer is sent and the seeker waits to see if, when and how the prayer is answered.

If you are accustomed to praying, it may be useful to know that **God may want you to do something** in order to make the prayer manifest. But how would you know what action you are supposed to take? One suggestion is that you can be listening with your intuitive ears to hear what God asks you to do.

What if you have difficulty believing that the Higher Power is always paying personal attention to you? I know many people who wonder if their prayers are heard. They think, *"God is so busy, how could He be listening to me?"* Does that describe you? If so, you may feel comfortable with having an angel or spirit guide that is within earshot and focuses solely on you. A personal guide can be a liaison between you and God. An angel or spirit guide can talk to you. Spirit guides can answer questions and provide assistance, on the spot.

After you send up a prayer to the Higher Power, you can then do a five-minute meditation and check in with your spirit guide or angel. You can ask what is wanted or needed from you in order to have your prayers manifested.

This gives you a direct, interactive communication with Spirit that is perhaps missing with prayer alone. This book introduces these actions to you in short and simple meditations that can take only five to ten minutes.

How a Guide Can Do God's Work

Sandra, age fifty, was very religious. She attended church regularly and prayed daily. Sandra had chronic pain in her back. She took pain medication but feared the long-term side effects. She began to pray for other methods of pain relief.

Perhaps in answer to her prayer, she was intuitively led to attend one of my workshops in which I taught meditations to meet spirit guides. Sandra learned how to meet various guides and how to communicate with them.

An intention is always set before going into a meditation. Sandra's intention was to meet a healing guide and ask for help to heal her back pain. In her healing meditation she met an angel. The angel informed Sandra that the emotional trauma of a past accident was still held in the cellular memory of her back.

The angel took Sandra back in time to a memory of when she fell off a horse at age 16. Sandra was shown a review of the entire incident as if she were watching a video. She saw that her teen-self was riding too fast and wasn't paying attention to the ground. She didn't see the big gopher hole. Sandra saw the horse trip and her younger self thrown onto the ground.

The angel told Sandra that her younger self was still stuck in that trauma. The cellular memory of the accident was still held in her back and that's why it still hurt now.

The angel showed Sandra the exact moment that needed to be healed. In this snapshot of time, she saw her 16 year old self lying on the ground in intense pain. In shamanic terms this is called "soul fragmentation." This means that her younger self was still there on the ground, forever stuck in that moment of trauma.

Up to now, Sandra had been reviewing the memory as if watching a movie. The angel now brought Sandra <u>into</u> the scene. The angel told Sandra: "You are the future self that is visiting the past self in order to rescue her. The angel then showed Sandra her healing color. She instructed Sandra to gather this color with her hands and put the color into the girl lying on the ground. Sandra gathered the healing color into her hands, and with gentle, soothing touch she put the color into her teen-self's back.

When that was completed, the guide suggested that Sandra talk to her younger self in calm, soothing tones and say: *"You are not seriously hurt. You are going to be all right. You can get up now."* Sandra's younger self got up off the ground, obviously feeling much better.

The guide then did something surprising. It told her younger self to get back on the horse and replay the scene with a different, positive outcome.

In the new version, the 16 year old atop the horse saw the gopher hole ahead of time. She reined in the horse, slowed it down and safely maneuvered around the hole. This time she did not fall.

With the help of her guide, Sandra had transformed the memory and released the emotional trauma that had been stuck in her body. Doing this allowed Sandra's back to fully heal. After this healing meditation, Sandra found that she was no longer in intense pain. She didn't need the pain medication anymore. This was the answer to her prayers.

This story demonstrates the great benefit in working directly with guides.

What else can a spirit guide do for you?

With the help of your guides you can ask for help on any matter and receive it. You can ask to release stress. You can ask for energy when you are feeling drained. You can ask for a healing intercession on any problem physical or emotional. All this and more is possible.

You can call on a guide in an emergency. As an example, I took my eighteen-year-old grandson to visit Sedona, a beautiful sacred place. We were climbing Bell Rock, one of the famous red rock formations said to be a spiritual vortex. We got almost to the top and then sat for awhile. My grandson told me about a problem he was having with a relationship. I suggested a certain meditation and led my grandson through it. In this meditative experience, a guide gave him knowledge about a past traumatic situation that had happened in a previous relationship. The guide gave him instructions for how to heal it. The guide told him that this would help release his fears and make his present relationship a lot better. That in itself was amazing.

When that meditation was completed, my grandson decided to climb to the top of Bell Rock. It was too steep for me, so I stayed where I was and did my own meditation. Some ten minutes later, I looked up to where my grandson had climbed. I saw him sitting on a rock outcrop with his eyes closed. Another ten minutes or so went by and then he opened his eyes and began the descent down to where I sat.

He told me an amazing story of what happened when he got up there. Just as he reached the top, he began to have an asthma attack.

This grandson has had asthma since age two. He had been hospitalized several times in the past few years with symptoms so severe he could not breathe, even with using his nebulizer (a machine that one uses to breathe in a mist of various medicines.)

My grandson lives at sea level. Here he was on top of this formation, at high altitude, with no emergency medicine and no cell phone. His nebulizer was back at the hotel. He had climbed up to the top too fast and that was too much exertion for his fragile lungs. He didn't want to call out and alarm me. He didn't think I could make it safely up to where he was to assist him. He figured that we were probably miles from the nearest emergency facility and he couldn't wait for a rescue. He needed help right now.

Because he had just done a successful meditation he decided he could do another one and ask Spirit for help. Gasping for breath, he sat down and closed his eyes. A guide began talking to him. It told my grandson to slow down his breathing. The guide then gave specific instructions for how to do so in a way my grandson had never before known was possible. After about ten minutes of listening to the guide's calming words and following what the guide told him to do, the asthma attack abated. He made it safely back down to me without my ever knowing the trouble he had been in. I was so grateful that I had taught him how to meditate and seek guidance that could be given on the spot.

How long does a guide hang out with you?

It is said that you have one main guide for your entire life. You also have numerous different guides throughout your life that appear when you need them and then leave when you no longer require their assistance. Their length of stay varies.

Some guides may stay throughout a long term project—such as writing a book. If there is only one book to be written, the guide will move on when it is completed.

The same guides may be with you for years supporting your passion, skill or talent, such as a person making a living as an artist, or as an author of many books. In these cases, guides can choose to stay long-term.

Other guides are very short-term. That is, they come to us for a present reason of need and leave when that need is fulfilled. For example, I once had a mirrored wall that I wanted to surround with a gilt frame, but I didn't know how to do the miter cuts. I called on a *carpenter guide* to show me how to do it. It turned out great. That particular guide appeared just for assistance I needed, then departed.

Are you ready to meet a guide?

The goal of this book is to enable you to see your guides, talk with them and work with them in a consciously-aware way. All the meditations will show how easy it is to <u>interact</u> with your guides.

Most of the meditations are in the last chapter. They all are designed to have you meet various kinds of guides. However, if you wish to meet one of your spirit guides now instead of waiting until you read the entire book, you can begin with the short meditation at the end of this chapter.

> *NOTE: if you have rarely or never meditated, read* Chapter 12, **"Preparing for a Meditation,"** *before doing this first one.*

When you do the following meditation, do not question the images you see. It is common to think you are making it all up. Just let that thought go. Relax and allow the experience to flow.

This is just a brief introduction to your guide. A more in-depth meditation for further interaction with this guide is in the last chapter.

Meditation

MEET AN IMPORTANT SPIRIT GUIDE

Intention: "I want to meet the spirit guide that I most need to know about right now."

1. Close your eyes. Take at least 3 deep, slow, clearing breaths.
2. Connect with your heart center by focusing on someone or something you dearly love. (Family member, pet, sunset, etc.)
3. Imagine you are in a safe, peaceful, place or landscape.
4. Ask for the guide you most need to meet right now.
5. How do you perceive it...Do you feel it? Do you see it?
6. Greet your guide. Feel its peaceful energy.
7. At this point, you can communicate with your guide.
8. Ask the guide: "What kind of guide are you? What do you do for me?

    How does the guide communicate with you?

    - Does it speak to you?
    - Does it show you things?
    - Does it take you on a journey?
9. Cup your hands and receive a gift from your guide. Take this gift and bring it in to your heart.
10. Return to the present. Bring your life force energy fully back in to your body.
11. Gently open your eyes. Record everything you experienced.

NOTE: Did this meditation work well for you? Did you have any problems tuning in to the guide?

If you are brand new to meditating, please understand that even short and simple meditations can take practice to achieve the desired result. Patience is recommended. Try this same meditation again at another time. When you do it the next time, relax. Don't try to force it.

If you did not see or experience anything, then please read on. There are many more hints and further instructions in the following chapters that can help you to be successful.

HINTS: You can memorize the steps to the shorter meditation, and then go on your visual journey. A meditation can work better when you have a friend or partner read the steps to you. Or you can record the steps and play them back.

Better yet, I can do this for you…

For a FREE audio recording of this meditation, go to Page 128, "RESOURCES. Type the URL for LINK #1 into your browser.

Chapter Three

ANGELS & SAINTS

Guardian Angels

Many spiritual traditions believe that you have a special type of spirit guide that is assigned to you on "the other side" before you incarnate. This same guide is said to stay with you for your entire life. In some religious traditions this guide is called a *guardian angel.* This is unique type of angel that is assigned to an earth soul and stays with that person until death. The guardian angel also accompanies the soul into the afterlife and helps the soul go to the Light. As the term 'guardian' indicates, this type of angel is there to serve and protect, to keep the soul safe and to offer guidance when needed.

When you call on your angel during a meditation, you can experience it in different ways. If you visualize easily, you will probably see an angel as you expect it to look. However, you may see only a bright light instead. This light may be golden or white, but could be any color. Once you become familiar with how you see your angel, it will usually look the same in every meditation.

People who do not visualize easily may feel the presence of the angel as perhaps a touch on the shoulder, or the brush of an angel wing. You could feel lightness in your heart, chest and shoulders. In all cases, the presence of the angel gives you a warm, peaceful and safe feeling.

No matter how you perceive your angel, do try to hear its message. This may come as a voice outside your head or as a thought within your brain. Your angel guide may give you its name if you ask. You can also ask questions and the angel will answer them.

Your own belief system will determine what kind of guides will come to you. If you believe in and trust the angels, you will certainly see an angel as your guide. However, be open to other types of guides that can assist for different wants and needs.

Both adults and children feel safe and comforted by angels. When one of my granddaughters turned five, I led her into a simple meditation to meet her spirit guide. She saw what she called her "special angel" and described this angel in detail. This granddaughter is now twelve and she tells me that she sees this very same angel when she closes her eyes and asks for advice.

A Quick Meditation

MEET YOUR GUARDIAN ANGEL

1. Close your eyes.
2. Take 3 deep, slow breaths.
3. Imagine a sacred or heavenly landscape.
4. Ask your guardian angel to appear to you.
5. Ask your angel: "What do I most need to know right now?"
6. Open your eyes. Record your experience.

Other types of angels

There is a range of angels in the hierarchy of the angelic realm, from the highest called archangels to the child-form called cherubim. Each of these types of angels are said to give unique types of guidance. In addition to your guardian angel, these other types of angels can appear to you when needed.

In the angel tradition, Archangels are the most highly evolved angels that one can call upon in specific circumstances. Archangel Michael may be one of the most well-known of that hierarchy of angels. Michael, a protector, is traditionally known as the *warrior* angel and is often pictured with a sword.

Saints

Saints also fill a big role in some religious traditions. However, saints are usually not thought of as personal guides that hang out with you. They are special holy spirits that can intercede on your behalf. Saints are souls who once had an earth life and spent much of that life in service to God in some way. Many of them were martyrs who were tortured and killed. Many died because they would not denounce Christ. In some religious traditions, at least two miracles have to be attributed to them after they died. Once these are proved by the church to be bona fide miracles, then the religious leaders can vote on canonizing a deceased soul as a saint. They are said to produce a miracle when a person fervently prays for one. There are hundreds of canonized saints and each one has a unique attribute, therefore an earth soul can pray to or call upon that particular saint for a specific purpose. For example, St. Christopher is the patron saint of travelers and is called upon to help a person travel safely. People who trust in St. Christopher to help keep them safe may wear a medal with his likeness or hang one in their vehicle.

Chapter Four

WISE BEINGS

One type of wise being is an evolved soul who no longer needs to be in a reincarnation cycle. Wise beings may have had earth incarnations as monks, teachers, healers, or had a spiritual focus. Another type of wise being is a highly evolved soul who resides in the higher dimensions, but never had an earth life.

If a spirit guide did have lifetimes on the earth plane, such a guide can look exactly as they appeared in one of their human incarnations. An example would be the highly evolved guide that came to Jane Roberts, author of the "Seth" books. When Jane began channeling Seth, she envisioned him the way he looked in his last earth incarnation—as a chubby-faced, bald man. Seth was a soul of profound intelligence, knowledgeable about quantum physics, the nature of the psyche and many other subjects. Through Jane's channeling Seth provided enough material to fill numerous books.

Sylvia Browne, a well-known psychic, and author of many books, consults with a guide who calls herself "Francine." Sylvia sees Francine as having a Hindu-like appearance. She wears loose clothing and has a long braid.

Jessed Ra is an Egyptian guide that I knew personally when we shared a lifetime in Egypt. He is my main writing guide. When he appears in a meditation, he looks exactly like he did in our former life. Jessed Ra was a high priest and scribe who worked in the library of Alexandria. He came to me at the very beginning of my dream work career when I began to write articles on dreams. He stayed on to assist when I began writing books. Along with Jessed Ra, I have also attracted a team of writing guides. Some of these come and go—depending on the particular subject I am writing about.

A spirit guide can take on a role for you

A spirit guide may choose to change his or her appearance to help you be more comfortable. If you feel more trusting of a guide who appears as a wise being in a long robe, then your guide may take on the wise-being image for you.

If you need to lighten up and have a sense of humor about your situation, your guide may appear in a form that makes you laugh. For example, my money guide is a leprechaun. I have been shown the wise-being likeness this guide normally adapts when I ask for other kinds of guidance. I do enjoy it though when this guide shows up in leprechaun guise when I do a meditation for manifesting money. It helps give me a sense of fun and lightness needed to overcome a block I may have on this subject.

Chapter Five

HIGHER SELF

Many people on the metaphysical or holistic spiritual path have a belief in what they call their "Higher Self." A H.S. is thought to be the highest spiritual part of your own, personal soul. It is an aspect of you that resides in a higher dimension. For that reason, the Higher Self is also called an *oversoul*.

In psychology terms the soul is divided into three levels: The subconscious, ego consciousness and the super-conscious. The term, *super-conscious* therefore, has the same meaning as *Higher Self*.

Your Higher Self is always with you because it is an integral part of your soul. Higher Self acts as your personal guidance system. H.S. can answer your questions, direct you in life, help you heal, provide profound spiritual dreams, and much more.

Because your H.S. resides in a higher dimension, it has an overview of your life path. It can *see* where you are headed and see who and what you might encounter and interact with. Your Higher Self is the aspect of you that continually sends guidance through your intuition. For this reason, it is well worth listening to.

For example: A few years ago at my workshop, "How to Listen to Your Intuition," a lady I'll call Barb told me this story:

I met a charismatic man at the restaurant where I worked. He came in every evening and sat at the bar section. I noticed him noticing me, so after my shift ended I began to stay for awhile and talk with him. I began to fall for his charm. One night on my drive home, I heard a loud voice speaking in my ear. The voice said: **"Don't you notice how much he drinks?"** *At that time I knew nothing about intuitive guidance. I ignored the warning. After a short dating period we moved in together. Three years later, after enduring nightly drunken stupors, and he had gone through all my savings, I finally got the courage to throw him out.*

When Barb finished her story, she told me how she wished she had listened to her intuition's warning in the first place. It would have saved her years of suffering and financial loss.

"Where" is your Higher Self?

You might be wondering where to find the Higher Self aspect of your soul. For some, this higher dimension exists within the body. If you have the belief that God is within, you may *see* inner sacred space as a special area within your heart. You might visualize this as an inner temple or some other structure that embodies sacredness. Or, you may envision your sacred place within as a ball of spiritual light. This can be any color, but is often either brilliant gold or bright white.

Others think of the Higher Self dimension as being above the body. In the experiences of the participants in my meditation groups, this Higher realm is anywhere from 3 to 30 feet above the head. Of course, it could be even higher up, depending on your beliefs. I recently heard a spiritual teacher say it was 300 feet up.

Distance is subjective. I suggest that you ask to be taken to the realm of your Higher Self and see for yourself where it is for you. If you believe it resides above, it's good to know that it is not that far from your body and effortlessly reachable.

If Higher Self is above, how do you get "there?"

You can easily arrive at this higher dimension by symbolic means. For example: Imagine that you are going up a wide curving stairway, or riding up in an elevator, or moving up on an escalator. Also, you can get there by being lifted as in a hot air balloon, riding on a cloud, or by simply floating up. Once you arrive at this higher place, your Higher Self will be there waiting to interact with you.

The realm of your Higher Self

The realm of the Higher Self can be something fantastical, majestic or magical–such as walking through an ancient forest filled with nature spirits, being among the stars in the universe, or exploring a crystal-laden cave. Or it can be more earth-like, such as walking through a beautiful garden, a forest, or a meadow filled with flowers. You might find yourself sitting next to a peaceful waterfall, or be on a mountain top. You could be within a structure such as a temple, cathedral or pyramid. The possibilities are vast, but it will always be a place that feels safe, serene and **sacred** to you. Don't have pre-conceived notions of what this realm will look like. Ask to go to the realm of Higher Self and let Spirit create it for you.

When I go to visit my Higher Self, she always appears to me in the same way. She wears a long, white flowing gown and an unusual headdress. She usually sits on a special stone throne in the middle of a Greek-style, open-air temple–complete with columns and a marble floor. Interestingly, although I dream in color and all my other visual imagery and meditations are in color, when I go to visit my Higher Self the entire experience is always in black and white. I believe that my Higher Self shows itself in this unusual way so I can be assured I am in the right place.

Your Higher Self is your manifesting guide

A Higher Self is confident, powerful, loving and generous. It wants you to ask for what you want and what you most need. It wants to provide, but it cannot give you what you don't ask for. Because you are born with free will, you do need to ask. Get into the habit of asking. This will serve you well.

You can make requests to your Higher Self through affirmations, vision boards, prayer, and of course–meditation. Do at least something every day to support your requests.

As stated in the books of numerous holistic authors—when you want to manifest something in your life, your Higher Self creates it first in that higher realm, then it can become manifest on the earth plane. As Richard Bach says in his book *Illusions*, "First imagined, then real." In order to manifest what you want, it is suggested that you must first imagine it, want it with all your heart, and then hand it over to your Higher Self to manifest it for you. This action is also known as "Let go and let God."

Your Higher Self is your healer

Because your Higher Self is the higher aspect of your soul, it holds the soul blueprint of a healthy body. Your Higher Self can help you heal. There is a meditation in the last chapter to meet your Higher Self. When you do the meditation, you can amend it to ask for healing.

Intuitive feelings can provide answer to your requests and quests for healing. Symptoms and feelings can help you discover emotions and memories stuck in your body that need to be released.

How a Higher Self can work with feelings and provide a healing

I taught my granddaughter how to meditate at an early age. As the years went by, I taught her how to meet specific guides appropriate to her age. When she was twelve I intuited that it was time for my granddaughter to meet her Higher Self.

We visited what I knew to be a portal, which is a gateway to other places. This can take a meditator to the past, into the future, or to other dimensions and realms. My granddaughter decided that she wanted her Higher Self to take her into the future. **Her intention was to meet her future self** who is doing well as she goes through her first year in high school. I had told her that a future self can also be a guide and provide the steps to success.

She closed her eyes and asked to go to her safe and peaceful place. She saw the familiar waterfall that she has gone to in past meditations. She then asked to meet her Higher Self. She was led behind the waterfall where she saw a welcoming cave filled with beautiful crystals. At first she saw a small child.

"You can't be my Higher Self," she said to the little girl standing in front of her.

The child then grew into a beautiful adult woman. "I **am** your Higher Self," she told my granddaughter. "I appeared first as a child so you would be comfortable with me." *(My granddaughter has a little sister that she adores.)*

My granddaughter told her Higher Self: "I want to meet my best High School future self. I want to find my future self who is doing well in my new school and is making good friends."

My granddaughter sat quietly with her eyes closed for a few moments. Then she said, "I have a feeling deep inside my lung." She gestured to the lower part of her chest.

The strongest way my 12 year old granddaughter receives her intuitions is through feelings. I have been teaching her how to translate what each feeling means.

To begin understanding a particular feeling, she needs to first ask: *Does it feel good or bad?* Then can then look into the feeling with her mind's eye and investigate it. If it's a good feeling it will tell her more about itself as a telepathic communication. If it's a bad feeling, she can go inside it to see what is held inside it.

So to begin this investigation of the feeling in her lung I asked, "Does it feel light? Does it feel positive?"

"Not really," she said. "It feels too tight."

"Look inside the feeling. What do you see?" I asked.

"I can't really see anything. It's just all black." she replied.

"Ask your Higher Self to shine a light into the blackness. What can you see when Higher Self brings in the light?"

"Okay," she replied. "My Higher Self brought in a beam of light."

She then told me what she saw within the tight feeling. It was a memory of something that had happened two years previously.

> *When I look inside the feeling, I see me about two years ago. I am at the shore of the lake. A boy came up behind me. I didn't see him. He pushed me hard and I fell into the lake. I wasn't expecting that. I swallowed water into my lungs.*
>
> *Now I am looking at the memory that happened a few days later. I got really sick with pneumonia.*

> *I hear the doctor saying, "From now on your lungs will be sensitive to smoke. You will probably have asthma from now on."*

She opened her eyes wide and looked at me. "Gosh Gram," she said, "I <u>have</u> been sensitive to smoke since then. I have been wheezy at times. I am on the volleyball team and sometimes it hurts my lungs when I play.

Obviously my granddaughter's lungs still held the traumatic memory of being pushed in the lake and then getting sick afterward. A part of her soul was still stuck in that memory. (In shamanic terms this is called *soul fragmentation*.) It is difficult for the body to heal completely when a trauma is stuck in cellular memory.

The doctor made it worse by telling her that bad things were going to happen to her lungs in the future. My mentor, Robert Dilts, a renowned NLP Master Trainer, calls these damaging statements "word viruses." Like a virus, negative words spoken aloud by a doctor to a sick person can spread into cellular memory. Every cell in the body can then 'believe' a dire prediction. *(For example, when a doctor tells a patient: "You have three months to live.")*

My granddaughter's intention in her meditation was find the most positive self she could be in High School. Apparently her Higher Self wanted her to heal this traumatic memory first. If she had not done so, she would have brought the doctor's dire prediction of an asthmatic condition into her future and been stuck with bad health. It might have prevented her from being on sports teams. Sports are so important to her.

Higher Self continued the meditation experience by explaining that my granddaughter could rescue her younger self from that stuck memory. It gave instructions for how to do it. My granddaughter was told to enter the scene and tell her younger self that she didn't have to stay at that lake anymore. Tell her that she was safe now and could leave that memory. (To take a younger self out of its moment of trauma is called *soul retrieval* in shamanic terms.)

My granddaughter went to her younger self, took her by the hand and brought her to her waterfall (her safe place). Her Higher Self then gave instructions for how to heal the memory. This is how my granddaughter was able to do it. In the original memory, she didn't know the boy was behind her. In the new version, she saw him and intuited that he was going to shove her. Instead of a fear-filled shock, it became a playful, fun, jump in the lake.

The bacteria in the lake may have caused the pneumonia. You can't change that. However, instead of a lingering illness, in the replay version she made it less of a problem and she recovered quickly.

On Higher Self's advice, my granddaughter then changed what the doctor had told her. In her revised version, the doctor said that she would recover completely and her lungs would be fine. No future problems. As a result, my granddaughter experienced a release of the tight feeling in her lung. She felt assured that smoke would no longer bother her in the future.

After the healing of that trauma, my granddaughter's Higher Self **then** could take her to meet with the best version of her future self. She sees herself getting good grades and meeting new worthwhile friends. Importantly, she sees herself in the future as healthy and able to play sports.

I want to emphasize that the healing that happened during this meditation was an unexpected surprise. It is an example of what can happen during a meditation when you are completely open and allow Higher Self or any spirit guide or power animal to take over the experience.

You can meet your Higher Self

I strongly suggest that in any meditation to meet your Higher Self that you ask it to appear to you in the form of a being. After all, it is a higher version of you, although more radiant, happy and at peace. Your Higher Self can have either a solid-looking image as if you were actually looking at a person, or its image can be ethereal (transparent).

In Chapter Nine there is a longer meditation designed to help you meet your Higher Self and enable you to communicate with this higher aspect of your soul. That meditation has suggestions designed to help you manifest what you desire. Please do amend it to ask Higher Self any questions you have, or to ask for healing.

In the meantime, on the next page is a brief version so that for now, you can simply meet and greet your Higher Self.

A Quick Meditation

MEET YOUR HIGHER SELF

Before you begin, examine your beliefs. Do you think that Higher Spirit is within you? Or, do you believe it is in a realm that is above you? Wherever you think it is, you should look directly at that place with your mind's eye.

Intention: To meet your Higher Self.

NOTE: You will want to envision your Higher Self as some sort of being so you can communicate with it.

1. Close your eyes.

2. Take 3 deep, slow breaths.

3. Depending on where you believe your Higher Self to be, either look within your heart, OR look above your head.

4. Allow the sacred realm of your Higher Self to flow into view.

5. Immerse yourself fully within this place. Breathe in the Light of it. Feel the peacefulness.

6. Ask your Higher Self to appear to you.

7. Ask your Higher Self to tell or show you what it most needs from you in order to always stay connected with this higher aspect of your soul.

8. Open your eyes and record your experience.

Chapter Six

ANIMAL GUIDES

Power animals

A power animal is a specific type of guide from the mammal, bird, reptile, or insect kingdoms. When an animal spirit guide appears, it offers you the essence of itself—its power *(i.e. strength, influence, assistance)*. An animal guide is both a provider and a protector.

Animal spirit guides appear to you exactly like they look in waking life. For example if your power animal is a bear, it will look like a bear. Some popular animal spirit guides are eagle, hawk, bear, wolf; and the big cats such as jaguar and panther. What you might think of as odd to be a power animal can be a powerful guide, such as snake, skunk, or spider. One of my unusual animal guides is a wombat.

How a power animal guide can help you

A power animal can come to you spontaneously in a meditation, a vision, or a dream. When you see one, you can ask the animal guide what its specific power is and what it can do for you.

Let us suppose that your power animal is a lion and it telepathically tells you that its power is courage. This lets you know that you that you have an ally on your life's journey for the courage to face your fears.

In a meditation you should always have an intention. You can then ask for a power animal that can assist with your intention. The animal that appears can communicate with you and answer questions. It may spontaneously take you on an experiential journey.

You can also merge with an animal when you need its power. To be one with the animal is feel its essence and borrow its power when you need it.

My wombat guide is interesting for a couple of reasons. One, for what he represents and another because he has such a sense of humor. I first met the wombat at a meditation workshop. When I saw this animal it was so strange looking, I had no idea what it was. So I asked, "What are you?" It replied, "I am the wombat." *(I had never seen one before and later looked this up in a book on Australian animals. Sure enough, he was a wombat.)*

I then asked, "What do you represent?" The wombat told me he was my power animal for invisibility. At the time, the wombat and its peculiar power seemed so strange to me that I questioned the vision and the animal's message.

A few weeks later I had an interesting dream: *I am riding up in an elevator. I sense something behind me and glance over my shoulder. In the back corner of the elevator I see what looks like a raccoon sitting up on its haunches. I turn and ask, "Who are you?" It took off its raccoon mask, held it up with a flourish and said, "I am the wombat in disguise." He then showed me how to put an energy shield around myself and my vehicle, much like the cloak of invisibility in the Harry Potter movies.*

Soon after having the dream, I saw the wombat again in a meditation. He showed me different scenarios in which invisibility could be useful, such as when I have to park in unsafe places, or when I want to go unnoticed in a crowd. That's when I knew for sure I could trust this little guy as a true power animal. I have used his energy shield many times since.

Different types of power creatures

There is a wide range of creatures within the realm of power animals. While any mammal including dolphins and whales may be a power animal, it can be any type of creature. It can be a bird such as a raven, hawk or an eagle. Or, it can be an insect, such as a spider, dragonfly or butterfly. A power animal can also be a mythical creature, such as a dragon, Pegasus or a unicorn.

Each animal that shows up at the start of a meditation journey has a special meaning for you. It is important to state your intention before you call on an animal spirit guide. Then, allow the particular animal that wants to fulfill that intention to choose you.

It is always a good idea to ask your animal what it stands for. Always ask what its particular power is. Also, be sure to ask what its job is for you on the meditation journey and afterward. For example, an animal's power could be *protection, wisdom, the ability to see within, lightheartedness* and so on. The possibilities are endless.

Medicine animals

In the Native American tradition, spirit animals are called *medicine* animals. There are books on this subject that tell you what the medicine (*the meaning, or the power*) is supposed to be for each animal.

One such system for understanding the medicine meaning of a power animal is called the Medicine Cards (*published by Bear and Company)*. This system includes a deck of animal cards and a book. Each card in the deck has an illustration of an animal or creature. The accompanying book gives the definition of the animal's medicine according to Native American tradition. These are valid beliefs from our ancestors and truths they lived by. Therefore, they may resonate with you.

One such example from the medicine system is the eagle. According to the belief system of Native American tribes: If eagle has chosen you, it is reminding you to take heart and gather your courage, for the universe is presenting you with an opportunity to soar above the mundane levels of your life. According to this tradition, eagle also teaches you to broaden your sense of self beyond the horizon of what is presently visible. To the Native Americans, eagle is the symbol for the Great Spirit. That is why eagle feathers are sacred to them.

Other definitions in the medicine animal system: Dog has the medicine of loyalty, bear provides introspection, whale is the record keeper, deer embodies gentleness and so on. You can use the Native American system to further understand the power of an animal that comes to you in a meditation. However, I include the caveat that your subconscious holds your own personal meanings about animals.

A meaning can change from the traditional, especially if you had a bad experience with a real life animal. When you were a child, if a vicious dog attacked you and you are still afraid of dogs, you are not likely to be comfortable with a dog as a personal power animal.

The animal you see in your meditation may, or may not mean what other traditions suggest. When an animal comes to you in a vision, have an open mind. Always allow the animal to show you or tell you what it means to you. If you do not immediately understand the animal's power, ASK it. If you do not get an immediate answer, use your intuition to help you comprehend its meaning.

What each power animal signifies for you could have a traditional meaning; or there might be a nuance of the traditional with an added meaning that is unique to you. Or, it can mean something totally unexpected—like my wombat.

Totem animals

You can have one or more power animals at any given time. Some stay longer term. Others can appear in our lives for a short period depending on what we need at a given moment. However, one animal in particular is said to be your totem animal.

Many people have a variety of animal spirit guides, however their totem animal is their main animal guide. Your totem is the animal that is with you for life, both in the spiritual and physical world.

You may encounter an animal while walking in nature and when it looks into your eyes, you intuitively <u>know</u> it is your totem guide.

My 12 year old granddaughter's totem animal is a deer. She saw a deer in a powerful dream when she was four. She has had close encounters with deer numerous times in waking life. Her daddy told me how she seems to call the deer to her. When they go camping there is always one that comes to the car.

In a recent meditation, a female deer spontaneously appeared. It told her that its power for her is *love* and it will help her to know how to have good relationships with family members. Right after this meditation, she and I were visiting in a rural town. In mid-day we drove around a corner and there stood a deer next to the road. I pulled up next to it and stopped the car. The deer looked at my granddaughte for a long while. Tears of *knowing* filled her eyes. Mine too.

Totem animals can be thought of as archetypal beings. The traditional meaning of the term "totem" goes back to tribal times. (As in *totem pole: a sacred tower of wood that has animal figures carved into it.*)

In modern cultures, some individuals—not otherwise involved in the practice of a tribal religion—have chosen to adopt a personal spirit animal helper which has special meaning to them. They may refer to this as a totem animal.

Although it is said that people may have many power animal guides but just one totem animal, those on the shamanic spiritual path may have several totem animal guides. A power animal can become your totem when it chooses you in a special dream, vision or meditation and does something very important on your behalf. A totem animal that appears in a dream is a very special gift. You are not likely to ever forget a powerful dream like that.

My totem animal is a jaguar. It originally came to me in this shamanic dream:

I meet Jaguar, my protective power animal

I am crossing a vast, African wild-animal park. I am alone and have nothing in my hands to protect myself.

I am about a third of the way across the veld (grassland) when I see a jaguar. It approaches me in a non-threatening manner. I am not afraid of it because it is purring. The jaguar gently jumps up into my arms. I'm surprised by how light it is. I continue my journey across the veld carrying the jaguar.

Suddenly, a herd of stampeding rhinos comes charging right at me. When the rhinos see the jaguar in my arms, the herd separates and each half of the herd veers off to either side of me—giving me a wide berth. A bit later, about twenty ferocious, snarling jackals run at me and circle me. When they see the jaguar in my arms they scamper off, whimpering. As I continue to cross the grassland this same kind of thing happens several times. Various dangerous animals approach but veer off when they spot the jaguar in my arms.

I get safely across the vast area. When I get to the opposite end of the veld, I gently put the jaguar down and crawl under a fence to safety. However, it does not leave. It continues to follow alongside me, like a faithful dog would.

When I awakened from this powerful dream I knew that the jaguar had chosen me and was now my totem animal. It is obvious from the dream that the jaguar is a protective spirit animal for me. It had come to me at that particular time because of a deeply-held fear I'd had of being out in the world. I had been programming dreams, asking Spirit to help me overcome this fear. The jaguar transformed the fear and gave me a feeling of safety. Since that dream, I can feel the jaguar's presence when I am out in the world in potentially unsafe places. I can sense it protectively circling me.

Have you ever had a special dream in which an animal appeared? Did it show you something? Did it do something for you? Has a particular animal shown up several times while you were out in nature? Did it look deeply into your eyes? Pay attention to the signs. You may have already met your totem animal. Tune into its power with the meditation in the last chapter.

Nature spirits and mythical creatures

Pegasus, fairies, elves, unicorns and dragons can appear as spirit guides, especially to children, but also to adults that love all things magical. Do these beings actually exist? If you call on a guide and see a mythical creature—can you trust that spiritual guidance can actually come through it?

I cannot say for sure that mythical creatures really do exist. Possibly somewhere, somehow—they do. It could be that a very long, long, time ago these creatures were present on the earth plane and their souls can now come back in spirit form. Or, perhaps there is an alternate reality, different from the one we reside in—a magical, spiritual realm or dimension where elementals are real.

It is also possible that a *wise-being guide* may choose to appear in one of these mythical forms to help an earth soul trust its wisdom. This would be as if a guide put on a costume, or is playing a role that makes the person feel safe and trusting of its messages.

I do know that mythical creatures can provide truthful, spiritual guidance. This is especially true for children. My grandkids are perfect examples of this. When each of them turned five, I taught them about spirit guides and how to meet them. I asked them to close their eyes and see the special *spirit-being* that is there to keep them safe. I explain that this is a guardian spirit who helps them and tells them things that feel right in their hearts. I don't pre-instruct the children about what they should see. I leave it up to each child to see, or imagine what will appear.

One of my grandsons had a magical dragon that would come to him each night just as he began to fall asleep. My grandson would climb onto the back of the dragon, which would then take him through a portal in his bedroom wall. Together they would ride into his dreams. They always flew over a magical landscape and then would drop down into a castle courtyard. While in the castle, the boy would see symbolic images or have metaphoric experiences. These would be different each time he visited that realm. Importantly, these dream experiences with the dragon helped him cope with some of the tough things that were going on in his waking life.

My youngest granddaughter, now age five, sees a pretty fairy in a pink dress. The fairy takes her to a safe place. She can talk to the fairy, ask questions and get answers that make sense to her. This could be her guardian angel in disguise because the child is familiar with fairies (and not with angels). However, it very well could be a special fairy guide because she is a magical child. She survived a series of life-saving surgeries just after birth.

One of the women in my shamanic journey group has a unicorn as her main guide. This guide has been appearing to her for years and has provided profound guidance that has helped her find and remove blocks and obstacles to her success.

Meet your power animal

You may have more than one power animal. At the present I have three main ones that have been with me for years. The power animal meditations can be done more than once to acquaint you with each of your animal guides.

There is an in-depth power animal meditation in the last chapter. If you are interested in meeting a power animal right now, the following short meditation is intended to simply acquaint you with a power animal.

Meditation

MEET A POWER ANIMAL

Intention: Ask to meet a power animal guide

1. Close your eyes.
2. Take at least 3 deep, slow, clearing breaths.
3. Imagine you are in a safe, peaceful place in nature.
4. Say: "I want to meet my power animal."
5. When you see it, ask it what it symbolizes for you. *(Example: Bear might mean strength. Owl could mean wisdom.)*
6. The animal gives you a gift. Take it into your heart.
7. Gently open your eyes. Record everything you experienced.

A meditation can flow better when someone reads the steps to you. I can do this for you. **Get an audio download of this meditation—absolutely FREE.**

Go to Page 128, "RESOURCES" and type in the URL for LINK #1 into your browser.

Chapter Seven

DECEASED LOVED ONES

The helper-spirit role of a dearly departed loved one

In metaphysical and holistic spiritual belief systems, a loved one who has crossed over is **not** called a *spirit guide*. If deceased loved ones come to you to provide help or advice, you can think of them as "helper spirits."

In order to be considered a true spirit guide, a soul has to be evolved to the point where it has learned all its life's lessons and no longer needs to reincarnate.

*(An evolved soul who is no longer in a reincarnation cycle **can** choose to come back to the earth plane to be a great teacher, wise prophet, or profound healer This could be considered a spirit guide in human form. Sometimes these are called "earth angels.")*

Sometimes a soul who is in-between lives in a reincarnation cycle chooses to be what I call a *helper spirit*. That role can be filled by someone we knew in this life who passed on. Or, it may be someone we knew in a past life who is not currently in a physical body.

A deceased loved one that is still in its reincarnation cycle can act as a spirit liaison or intermediary for either a higher evolved guide, one's Higher Self or the Higher Power. In other words, a *helper spirit* is being guided by a *more-*

evolved spirit guide. A helper spirit cares about you and wants to be of assistance when you are in need.

A deceased person can indeed be considered a soul in spirit form. As such, a departed soul can then be a *helper spirit* and provide advice to the living.

The question here is do you want that? If your deceased mom, dad, grandparent, spouse or friend was difficult to be around in life, will they be enlightened enough on the other side to offer quality support?

Here are ways to think about this. If departed souls were able to go immediately into the Light, they are with their Higher Self, their guides and angels, and most probably other relatives and pets who died before they did.

Even a person who had a tough life is able to get help to release emotional baggage, but that doesn't happen immediately after death.

Souls who have gone into the Light must still go through an orientation. They are taught by guides how to maneuver in the afterlife. For positive transformation to occur, the soul in transition must be able to listen to the guides and follow their direction. If and when that transpires, the deceased loved one may then decide to "visit" you and apologize for the way he or she treated you. This will feel sincere. It can generate a healing of a hurt relationship deep within your soul.

Not all souls immediately go to the Light after death

Souls can get stuck in the astral plane (a lower dimension than the Light), or hang out in the place where they died. This can happen for a number of reasons.

If a person died in a depressed, emotional state of mind, a soul can get stuck on either the earth plane or in the astral plane. Negative emotional states are brought into the afterlife and are so heavy that a deceased soul can get bogged down. They perhaps cannot see the Light or be able to reach it without help.

Robin Williams's movie "When Dreams May Come" is an example of how that can happen. In the movie, his wife died in a state of despair because her children had previously died in a tragic accident. In her version of the afterlife she could not see the happy souls of her children because of her despair. A scene in the movie showed her slumped over with eyes downcast. She was in an afterlife version of her earthly home, however it was in a state of rack and ruin *(reflecting her emotional state)*. Her husband (Robin's character) was able to rescue her with the help of their son's spirit. However, it was not easy.

A person who committed suicide to escape the depression of life can certainly take that depressed emotional state into the afterlife and be stuck in it until guides can get through for rescue. Again, a difficult task.

A soul may not get to the Light if the person was murdered or killed in an accident and the soul left the body suddenly. A good example of this is the movie "The Sixth Sense" in which Bruce Willis's character was shot, but doesn't realize he is dead until the end of the movie.

Another reason is that sometimes a person does not know that he or she died. This can happen if a person died in their sleep or died while they were in a coma. It can be truly confusing for the soul if death happened unbeknownst and the person awakens in the spirit body, (which is perceived as it looked in waking life).

A person might not know they are dead if they died under the influence of drugs. This can happen with any type of drug overdose—whether they were bought illegally or were prescribed by a doctor. It is well-known that accidental overdoses happen in hospitals. People who die in a morphine-induced state and who had not been properly prepared for death by a hospice team, could wander in a confused state in the afterlife.

Sometimes there is unfinished earth business, such as in the movie "Ghost" in which Patrick Swayze's character had to protect his wife from the man who murdered him.

The TV series "Ghost Whisperer," with Jennifer Love Hewitt, had what I believe to be accurate accounts of the many reasons an earth soul can get stuck and not get to the Light. Jennifer's character was skilled in helping these stuck souls. There actually are people on earth who have this ability to send souls to the Light.

If departed loved ones did not get to the Light and they hang around, their communication may be similar to the way they were in life, which may be critical, judgmental, etc. In that case you probably won't want to listen it them. If any communication from *the other side* makes you feel bad, it is not true spirit-helper guidance.

If, however, you had a <u>good</u> relationship with your loved one and sense that he or she did not get to the Light, you can help. Perhaps you are the one hanging on because of intense grief. What is needed is to tell the departed loved one: "I am going to be all right. It is okay for you to leave now." Say to the soul "I release you. I can let you go, because I know you can come back to me after you get to the Light. It is true that when the soul gets into the Light, it can then come to visit with you afterward at any time. That is a better situation for the both of you.

Another thing you can do for stuck souls is to call on other relatives that previously passed on to come and escort them to the Light. If your loved one had a religious belief, such as in Jesus, you can ask Jesus to come and help. If they believed in angels, then call on the angels.

Helper spirits are in the Light

When loved ones choose to be *helper spirits*, they can bring spiritually-led advice from an evolved spirit guide. They can act as a liaison or intermediary between you and a spirit guide of higher vibration, especially if your vibration does not yet match the energy of a highly evolved guide. A helper spirit can pass along messages from a guide of higher vibration who cannot yet get through to the earth soul.

Communication from a departed loved one can happen in dreams, during a meditation, or you can hear the message as a telepathic whispering in your mind. You may have already experienced this after a loved one died.

Another reason for a deceased family member to come back to you in the form of a liaison or spirit helper is that you may be more comfortable getting guidance from someone you already trust.

For example, my beloved grandmother, who had died twenty years previously, was asked to be a liaison for a higher evolved guide for my benefit. In the first chapter of this book I told the story of a dream in which my grandmother appeared. She came to tell me that I could help my mom heal and drive again. I trusted her so much when she was alive, that I totally believed her afterlife message.

In subsequent dreams she told me that she was chosen as a spiritual liaison because I had trusted her so much when she was alive. She said that I could trust the information that the higher guide had given her to pass along to me. Grandma stayed with me for over six months as this intermediary, until my trust level and my vibration raised high enough to be able to get direct communication from the higher evolved guide.

During that period I received messages from my grandmother in numerous dreams. She also came to visit while I was awake. She would get my attention in various ways. For example, I would smell her perfume in the air.

Or, hear her voice in my ear. I inherited pieces of her jewelry and sometimes I would find her earring on my pillow. When any of these occurred, I knew to stop what I was doing, clear my mind, and LISTEN.

Because of these experiences with the spirit of my grandmother, I knew the "other side" was much more interesting and had much more happening than I was led to believe from religious teachings. Several years after her helper spirit role was completed, Grandma told me that she loved what I was learning about healing so much that she is now in a school to be trained to be a healer in her next life.

Preparing a dying loved one for the afterlife

I previously mentioned that a deceased person goes through an orientation to learn how to maneuver on *the other side*. Because I know what can be done after arriving in the afterlife, I gave each of my parents pre-instruction before they died. When they were in their last months of life, I traveled to the Midwest and stayed for months so I could "hospice" them. We thoroughly discussed the afterlife experience. I taught them what they could expect and what they could achieve.

If you are interested in pre-planning your own after-death experience, or want to help a dying loved one have a loving and safe entry into the afterlife, a great book on this subject is *Going Out in Style, a Guide to Planetary Departure,* by Marcia Beachy.

Here is just a bit of what I did for my dad. When he was dying he was very upset because he wanted to continue helping people like he did in life. I told him that he could appear in his family's dreams whenever he wanted and give his advice. I also told him that he could visit me during my waking day and whisper the special nickname that only he called me. I promised I would hear him and we could talk.

He passed in the year 2000. Immediately after his death, he began appearing in two of my grandsons' dreams. He told them he would teach them how to be a success in business. To this day he comes often to visit me. In some of my dreams a door will suddenly fly open and he strolls right in. Or, at times when I am awake, I will hear his voice in my ear, addressing me by the special pet name he called me in life. It is so comforting to be able to communicate with him and get his sage advice. He truly is a helper spirit.

Mom relished the vacations we took in the later years of her life. We took a three-week vacation every year for twelve years. We traveled the world together. She loved Hawaii so much that we went there every two years. When she was dying at age eighty-seven, I told her she could do anything she wanted in her afterlife. I mentioned what Dad was doing and suggested that she could do the same. But Mom didn't want that role. She had been stuck in a wheel chair since she had turned eighty and could no longer travel. She said that after she died she wanted to be on an endless vacation. She wanted to go to Hawaii and sit on a patio watching the ocean. She also wanted to have a table full of Chinese food—her very favorite.

In Mom's afterlife, that is exactly where she is. A few days after Mom died, I asked my spirit guide to let me know if she got to her afterlife version of Hawaii. Still in her home, I fell asleep on a bed in her spare room. In the middle of the night I awakened with my spirit guide's voice telling me to reach down into a box on the side of the bed. I did so and had what felt like a small photograph in my hand. I turned on the light and looked at it. From within the photo, I saw her waving at me. It was a snapshot of her in a Hawaiian garden, a picture I had taken on one of our trips. "Wow!" I said in amazement. "Mom made it there, and in record time." Mom is not in the actual Hawaii on the earth plane. Rather she is in a created version of what we might think of as the heavenly realm.

Unlike my dad, Mom's spirit-self doesn't come to visit me. Instead, while in meditations, my Tibetan guide will sometimes surprise me and take me to see her. I always find her sitting on a patio, blissfully gazing at the ocean. The table is laden with every kind of Chinese food possible. When I appear at her side, she always looks up and greets me the same way: "Hi Honey. Sit down. Have something to eat." (We are Italian.) Then she will ask me to take her on a trip. I ask her where she wants to go. Then I take her by the hand and my guide flies us to the place of her choosing. Afterward, I return her to her beachside table. The meditation ends there and I come back to my present reality. Is this real? Yes, definitely! I have been given proof in so many ways.

I didn't always have a good relationship with my mom. In life, she had a need for control and could be difficult to be around. Because of my instruction, she went immediately into the Light and has a changed personality. She is pleasant and always speaks to me in a kindly voice tone. I do believe this happened because she was fully prepared for how to have a positive afterlife, and <u>is</u> having one. She has no inclination, yet, to provide advice. All she wants to do is enjoy her endless vacation. I am happy for her.

You may or may not want to invite participation from a deceased family member or spouse. If he or she was unkind to you, that energy may have been carried into the afterlife, at least for awhile.

However, if you had a good and loving relationship with a parent or spouse who passed on, you might want to invite the soul of that person to visit with you. You can do this for a pet as well. If your loved ones were wise and possessed advice you would welcome, then you can also ask them to be *spirit helpers* for you.

DREAM PROGRAM

Ask a dearly departed loved one to visit you

Dream request: Before falling asleep, ask Spirit:

"Please bring my loved one, ___(name)___, to visit me."
Add: "I want to remember my dream."

If your guide tells you that it is unlikely at this time for the departed loved one to come to you *(as in my mom's case)*, then ask your guide to take you to visit that person—wherever he or she is.

You can also do a meditation to meet with a departed loved one. There is one for this purpose in the last chapter.

Chapter Eight

SPIRIT GUIDES IN DREAMS

This Practical Guide teaches you how to call on spirit guides to appear in a daytime meditation.

It is also possible for guides to come into your night time dreams. When you ask for help—it can be provided both by day and by night.

Many times, a guide that appears in a dream will take the form of an assistant who comes along when you most need one. In my dream support groups, numerous individuals have shared dreams in which a guide appeared as either a helpful policeman, a construction worker that repairs something, a teacher, a waiter, a crossing guard—and so on.

An example of how a dreaming guide works

One of my clients had been terribly hurt, financially, in a stock fraud (Ponzi) scheme. This stock broker defrauded her and numerous others of their life savings. Because the broker had been her good friend, she felt betrayed and went through years of emotional pain.

During these years, she had a recurring nightmare in which the foundation to her house was falling apart. In each dream, she tried using tools to repair it but the tools were never the right ones. So no matter how she tried to fix the problem, she could not.

She met me one day through mutual friends and heard that I helped people with their nightmares. Using my Dream Decipher Process, I helped her interpret the dream. She discovered that it addressed the bitterness that was stuck deep within. The dream's message was that this betrayal had damaged her to the foundation of her soul.

Per my instructions, she started asking–before she fell asleep–for a dream to help her let go of her bitterness. One night the dream changed. A construction worker suddenly appeared with the correct tools. She watched while he repaired the foundation for her. In this new dream version, her guide appeared in the guise of a repairman to show her that spirit help was being provided and that the hurt held deeply in her subconscious was being healed.

When any kind of assistant shows up in a dream and provides either a positive message, actually helps you out with something, or repairs something—you can trust that it is a spirit guide, Higher Self, angel, or other emissary of Spirit coming to your aid.

There are many accounts in my book, *Decipher Your Dreams*, about the guidance that is provided when a person requests it before falling asleep.

You can ask for a guide to come to your aid in your dreams. This is a technique called dream programming or intentional dreaming.

How to program a dream:

Before you fall asleep state your intention. Focus on what you want for a few moments. See it happen. Feel how good it will feel when it does happen.

Then request to have this happen in your dreams. Ask your guide to work on this for you while you are asleep. Do this program at least three nights in a row.

You do not have to remember your dreams for this to work. All you need to do is keep asking for help. Have faith that you will receive what you want or need.

If you do **not** remember a dream during the three nights of programming it is perfectly ok. During the next few days though, be alert for how your request is answered. You may be led to a certain book, or person, or place that provides exactly what you need. Be patient. If no results happen in three nights of asking, then continue the exact, same program for a week.

As an example of how this can work: A friend had an accident and totaled his car. The insurance company claimed that (according to their computer) he was not insured. They insisted that he had dropped the coverage. The glitch apparently happened when his girlfriend bought a new car and he called the insurance company to add her car to his policy. Somehow the computer added her new car, but dropped his.

The man was in my dream group, so I suggested he program a dream and ask a guide for help. He did so for three nights in a row. He did not remember any of his dreams, but he kept requesting help. On the fourth morning an acquaintance he hadn't seen in years spontaneously stopped by his house telling him that she had a sudden thought to come and visit him.

During their catch-up conversation he mentioned his insurance dilemma. She told him that she used to work in the insurance field. She asked if his insurance company had mailed him a *Declaration of Insurance* when he had paid the bill. He went to his file and found it. His friend said, "This is like gold. It proves they insured your car. Fax them a copy." He did so. The insurance company honored this proof and paid him full value for his lost car. He knows the Universe responded to his dream request and sent this knowledgeable lady over to see him.

The members of my dream group have had great results requesting Spirit's help before going to sleep. This has happened for me so many times I have lost count. Just one major example: In the early eighties, I had been doing extensive dream research. I could not find a valid method for dream interpretation that worked. So I began programming dreams, asking Spirit for an interpretation method that I could teach to others.

In 1985, I had a dream in which a shaman guide gave me the "Dream Decipher Process." I awakened from a dream with all the steps to the process clearly in my mind. Since that time, this method has never failed to give the accurate meaning of dreams for the thousands of people who have used it.

There are guides for everything

What do you want to accomplish? What do you want to manifest in your life? As stated before—there are guides for everything.

When you do a meditation to manifest something, it is important to **also make the exact, same request before you fall asleep each night.** While you are lying in bed, review the imagery you saw in your meditation. Ask your guide to send this imagery into your dreams and to continue the dreaming quest every night while you are asleep.

You do not have to remember any dreams to get great results. Just keep asking every night before you fall asleep. By doing this you are reprogramming your subconscious to transform your limiting beliefs and allow more into your life.

Pay attention to what happens during the next few days. What happens that may answer your request? It could be a call from someone or you run into the precise person you need. Or, the right book or newspaper falls into your hands. Spirit **will** answer your requests in some way. You may already have experienced something like that. If so, this is proof that guides are at work on your behalf!

If you are interested in dreams, dream programming, and dream interpretation, my comprehensive book titled: **Decipher Your Dreams, Decipher Your Life** is available on Amazon.com. You can use the "search inside" feature to peruse it.

Because I chose a path as a healer, spiritual teacher and writer, my guides are such an important influence in my work. I have four shaman spirit guides that have been working with me for almost three decades. They come to me both in dreams and in meditations.

My Higher Self encouraged me to write a book called: **Shamanic Dreaming**. This book focuses on programming dreams for self-healing. It also shows you how to make dream requests to help others. There is a chapter for how to help the planet overcome its problems of tree loss, global warming, contaminated waterways, etc.

To order this book, see information on 129 "RESOURCES."

Chapter Nine

PERCEIVING YOUR GUIDES

Guides may want you to see them as they had looked when they lived on the earth plane. This is especially true of healing guides who actually were healers in many of their earth incarnations. Some of the healing practitioners in my shamanic journey groups have seen Native American medicine men or women, or shamans from other cultures as their guides. One has a Tibetan monk as a teacher.

If you want a serious-minded guide, ask for one. A *Wise-being guide* usually has a persona that befits its role, such as a having a wizened-looking face, perhaps wearing a long robe. Or, a guide can be in the raiment of its culture—such as the white deerskins, beads and feathers of the medicine woman.

How does a guide communicate its message?

Guides can be clever indeed and communicate in any number of ways. A guide can decide to come as a symbolic form or shape. For example, David, one of my teen clients, hated school and had poor grades—mainly D's and F's. I led him through a meditation to call on a motivation guide. This guide chose to appear to David in the guise of a basketball.

This sports-focused guide told David that his poor grades were keeping him off the team. The guide gave him this message: *"Put in the effort to at least make C's, and school will become fun again because you will get to play sports."* Through the weeks, his guide continued to whisper in David's ear about playing sports. This did motivate him to put in the effort to bring up his grades. A basketball as a guide may seem very odd, but to David it made perfect sense. When it comes to a guide's appearance—whatever is logical to you is how you will perceive your guide.

In an effort to have you lighten up, a guide can be full of fun and show itself as an image that embodies humor. For example, a friend of mine sees one of her guides as a gangly, cartoony dancing frog. It wears a top hat, a formal black coat with tails and a bowtie. The frog twirls a black, shiny staff with a large crystal on top. As she watches, the frog dances his way up a wide-winding stairway to the tune of "Putting on the Ritz." The stairway leads up to the realm of Higher Self and her sacred place. The frog usually appears for her in meditation when she feels bogged down with stress. This guide always makes her laugh and that shifts her into a more positive state.

Most people tend to have negative thoughts a lot of the time. This is common in our stress-filled life. This is detrimental thinking. When you constantly think negative thoughts, bad feelings get stuck in your body. Stress, worry and fear can get trapped in your body, which could create illness. A guide, therefore, may show you one or more happy memories. By providing these, a guide is showing you that having positive feelings is beneficial for you. A positive memory that makes you smile actually does transform negativity that has been stuck within you.

Some guides show you things in metaphoric form, such as a scene with some kind of action happening. For example, a student in my study group asked to understand why she couldn't bring herself to finish a book proposal. She went through an energy drain whenever she tried to work on it. She felt stuck and overwhelmed.

In our meditation study group, I led a meditation designed to ask a guide the reason for a personal problem My student's intention was to ask the guide's help for the overwhelm that occurred when she tried to write her proposal.

In her meditation, she was taken into a scene where two sides were at war. A cannon was shooting cannon balls at someone on the far side of a vast meadow. Because of the type of cannon, the civil war came to mind.

By interpreting this scene intuitively using my Dream Decipher method, she learned that two parts within her subconscious were at war. One part wanted her to write the proposal, but the opposing part was trying to shoot it down. She heard this part say: *Writing it was too hard, so why bother?*

After she intuited the situation and learned why the two parts of herself were at war, an angel suddenly appeared in the sky. The angel held a white flag. The angel floated down into the middle of the field and obviously called a truce. With the angel's help, both sides of the problem came together and ended the inner war. As a result, the woman was able to get the proposal finished before the deadline.

I had mentioned my leprechaun *(money guide)* earlier. He never says a word. Instead, he holds up a sign. The message on his sign changes each time I see him. This is the way he has chosen to communicate with me. I must read what it says on the sign to know what he wants me to do to manifest extra income. For example, in one meditation his sign read: *"Finish the book."* I *had* been procrastinating. This short and firm message gave me the kick in the pants I needed.

A guide may communicate by showing symbolic images and forms. For example: A person may ask for strength to go through a tough situation. The guide may then show symbolic images of strength, such as *barbells* or a *weight lifter.*

Chapter Ten

THE SCIENCE OF PERCEPTION

How your brain processes a meditation experience

Messages from guides are received through your intuition. You may not believe you are intuitive. You can let go of that belief right now. You are simply unfamiliar with how intuition works.

Everyone is intuitive. You were born with this ability. There has to be a connection to Source/Spirit for your health and well-being. Intuition is this connection. There are neural pathways in the brain that connect to intuitive senses. They don't need to be activated, they are already working quite well. All you have to do is recognize how.

Guides can communicate in a number of ways. How you perceive their communications will depend on the main modality (sense) in which you normally receive intuitions.

The three major intuitive modalities

- Visual (*seeing images that Spirit provides*)
- Auditory (*hearing what a spirit guide has to say*)
- Kinesthetic (having a *feeling of rightness* about the guide's message).

Primarily, your brain uses one of these senses to process intuited information. In other words, you are mainly either a **visual,** or an **auditory,** or a

kinesthetic processor. However, you do receive intuitions in the other two senses as well, albeit not as strongly.

Visual intuitions: If you are primarily a **visual** person, then with eyes closed you should easily envision the safe place suggested in the meditations. You will also see your guides clearly. For those who visualize easily, a guide can look solid as if it had a body. Or a guide might appear as an ethereal (transparent) figure. Or, you may perceive a guide as moving energy. Guides can also appear in the form of one or more colors.

Auditory intuitions: If you are primarily **auditory** you will clearly hear the guide speaking to you. You will perceive the voice of the guide either just outside your head, or hear its message as a telepathic communication. The "knowing" comes as thoughts going through your head.

Kinesthetic intuitions: If you are mainly a **kinesthetic** perceiver, you will definitely feel the presence of a guide. You may get a feeling when the guide is near. You may perhaps feel the guide's touch—as if a hand is touching your cheek, or an angel wing is brushing your shoulder. You should feel as if you are held safe. Kinesthetic perceptions of a guide's message can come as goose bumps, or tingles down the arms or spine, or as energy moving up in your body, or a warm all-over feeling. You may feel lighter and uplifted.

Even if your strongest intuitive modality is either your visual or auditory sense, almost everyone has a kinesthetic component to intuition as well. In other words, what the guide shows you, or what the guide tells you will *feel right* in a particular spot in your body.

Many kinesthetic-intuitive people say they get a "gut feeling." Interestingly, after doing my Intuition Location-Finder Exercise, this spot is rarely found in their gut. Rather, they find that the feeling-spot of intuition is either in the heart; at a spot slightly above the heart; to the left or right of the heart nearer the shoulder; or, just below the heart. There are other common places for this intuitive spot—such as the throat, or just above or at the stomach. You can do the exercise at the end of this chapter to be sure where your *feel right spot* is.

As stated above, most people receive an intuition mainly through one sense in a stronger, more noticeable way. However, in addition to your main intuitive perceptual sense, you do also receive that same intuition through your other two senses. Intuition and Spirit guidance is actually sent to all three senses simultaneously. This happens so quickly that the intuitions received in the other two subtler senses are usually not noticed.

If one of your three senses is too subtle to be recognized, your guide will find a way around that. For example, you may visualize easily but have a problem with hearing the guide's message. To help you understand its message, the guide may show you metaphoric scenes (much like in a dream), or it may flash a series of symbolic images. Pay attention if that happens. It is important communication. Record what you see. All imagery can be deciphered afterward.

If you do not visualize easily, your guide may instead converse with you, or perhaps use feelings to communicate.

What if feelings are the only thing that happens in a meditation?

There are some people who do not see images at all when their eyes are closed. Instead they may only feel their intuition. If that is your case, then you should ask, "What is this feeling trying to tell me?" Tune into it. You can ask a feeling to tell you about itself. Relax and let the thoughts flow into your mind. Feelings can be given a voice and say what a guide wants you to know.

Intuitive feelings can have important guidance to impart in answer to your requests and quests. If a feeling is the only thing that happens in a meditation, you can try this technique: Discern exactly where the feeling is. Check for it in your body. If it's not in the body, look for it in the brain.

Pretend you have x-ray vision. Focus directly at the spot where the feeling is strongest. Ask: What does this feeling want to tell me? Thoughts will pop into your mind. They may be subtle. Make them louder. It may seem like you are just talking to yourself. Let this go and simply allow the communication to continue.

Feelings can help you discover emotions and memories stuck in your body that need to be released. If the there is a feeling in your body that feels tight, or is a bit painful, you can ask: "What is held inside this feeling? Travel inside it with your mind's eye. At first you might only blackness or darkness. If that happens, ask your spirit guide to shine a light into it. Breathe slowly, relax. Keep asking to know what is inside the feeling. You may see an image. If not, ask the feeling to tell you about itself.

NOTE: Review the story in the last part of Chapter Five about my granddaughter's experience of being thrown into the lake and getting pneumonia afterward. **By looking into the "tight" feeling in her lung,** *she found this trauma and with the help of her Higher Self, she healed it.*

Help for problems with seeing meditation imagery

When people close their eyes to meditate they expect to see images the way they do in real life. That is—a scene out in front, large as life, in full color and perhaps with some movement. Some <u>do</u> see in that way. But many don't. Images can be fleeting. They are there one moment and–poof–gone the next. Or, they may blink on and off. Some people do not see in color. They may see only shades of grey, or sepia tones. Images can be solid, or transparent. Or they may be just outlines like a line drawing.

Importantly, some people do not see things out in front of them at all. Rather they see the images on the inside of their forehead, behind their eyes, or, somewhere within the brain. As you will learn later in this chapter, it is important to direct your eyes to the exact spot where images appear in order to see them.

When I began to meditate, I did not see much at all when I closed my eyes. By doing the Visual Imagery Exercise (given below) I began to notice that images were there, but not where I had expected them to be. Also, they didn't look how I expected them to look. My images were very tiny *(an inch high)* and only in my peripheral vision, about an arm's length away. They were a transparent, ghostly white. They blinked on and off. Worse, they disappeared if I looked directly at them for more than a few seconds.

Luckily, I had already created my *Voice of Intuition Exercise*, and so I knew where to look to access my intuitive voice. I found that I could rely on my Voice of Intuition to give expanded information about the little I could see. By frequently doing short meditations I was eventually able to open my visual imagery in wondrous ways. I now see bright colors. My images are also big as real life and they stay stable.

If you do have a problem perceiving the guided imagery suggested in the meditations, have patience. Do the exercise below. It is designed to acquaint you with **how** you see images when your eyes are closed.

Once you discover where you see imagery, it is important to direct your eyes to that location while doing a meditation. Looking at the spot with your eyes closed opens the neural pathway to your visual intuition.

- If you see out in front of you, then LOOK out in front.
- If you see on the inside of your forehead, then LOOK there for the images.
- If you discover that you see your images in a certain spot inside your brain, then LOOK at that spot for the suggested imagery in the meditations.

Exercise

HOW YOU SEE WITH YOUR MIND'S EYE

It helps to know **how** you see by visualizing something that you are familiar with. Use your imagination. Close your eyes and pretend you can see the following suggested images:

Imagine that you are standing at the door to your bathroom and are looking into that room. Take your time. Look around slowly. Focus on each of the familiar objects in the room. Towels, tub, toiletries sink, etc.

<u>Where</u> do see the image of the bathroom?

- Is it out in front of you?
- Or do you see it on the inside of your forehead?
- Or behind your eyes?
- Or in your brain?

Check for color:

- Are the images in natural color? *(As in real life)*
- Or in subdued colors?
- Or are they in black and white, or subtler shades of grey?
- Or are they in sepia-tones?

Are the images solid looking? Or are they transparent?

Focus on one object in the bathroom.

- Does the image stay?
- Or, is it there for a moment, then disappear?
- Or, does the image blink on and off?

Pretend that you have turned on the water in the sink and put the plug in.

Is there movement, as if you are watching a movie? If so…

- Is the water flowing?
- Do you see the sink fill with water?

Or is it a still picture, like a snapshot? If so…

- Is it just one snapshot?
- Or do you see a series of snapshots?
- Are they framed?
- or unframed?

This exercise should show you exactly HOW you see with your eyes closed. You can use this information to become comfortable with how you see imagery in the suggested meditations in the last chapter.

Reminder: When you are doing a meditation, direct your eyes to the location where you see imagery with your mind's eye. This creates a strong neural pathway connection that enables you to visually perceive your guides and see what they want to show you.

Chapter Eleven

INTUITION LOCATION-FINDER EXERCISE©

Recognizing how you perceive intuitions

Your *Voice of Intuition* is verbal communication from Spirit. Intuitive guidance can come through an angel, a spirit guide, God, Higher Self or power animal. If you do not have a belief in a Higher Power, then consider that your intuition could stem from a deeper, all-knowing aspect in your psyche.

No matter what you believe about the source of your intuition, It is important to have an interactive relationship with it. The beauty of this is that you can get the guidance you seek—on the spot—whenever you ask for it.

Your intuition is the gateway for guides to come through to you. Developing your intuitive ability can be done with my "Intuition Location-Finder Exercise" coupled with my "Dream Decipher Process." With these intertwined methods you can clearly interpret all symbols and metaphors—whether they are seen in meditations, or in dreams.

Symbols must be interpreted intuitively to make accurate sense of them. Your intuition is the key to help you understand symbolic images and discover exactly how they answer your requests.

About the "Intuition Location-Finder Exercise"

You are born with specific neural pathways that connect with the Source of your intuition. The "Intuition Location-Finder Exercise" is a technique that shows you how to find the exact location where intuition *feels right* in your body.

Importantly, this exercise also shows you how to pinpoint the specific spot where you hear your Voice of Intuition. *(This spot is almost always found somewhere in or near the head.)*

You may not always be in a private place where you can get guidance in a meditation—even a five-minute one. You can get clear and strong communication from a guide or your Higher Self with your eyes open. When you know specifically <u>where to look</u> to have the neural pathway connection to your guides, you can direct your eyes to that spot at any time that you want an instant answer to any question, on demand!

The intuition exercise takes only minutes and needs to be done only once. After you have discovered the exact spot where you hear your intuitive voice, a simple, directed eye-movement to that spot is all it takes to connect with your intuition throughout a meditation.

It would be beneficial to do the **"Intuition Location-Finder Exercise"** before you do the meditations. Your guides come through your intuitive pathways. If a guide shows you a symbolic image, you might not understand the meaning of what you are seeing. In that case, you can direct your eyes to the location where you hear your intuitive voice. Intuition will interpret the meaning of the symbol for you.

Learning how to access your intuitive voice also helps to accurately and clearly hone in on the guide's message when it is given in metaphor, or story form.

Your Voice of Intuition can tell you what you are looking at if you cannot see meditation imagery clearly or if you have trouble visualizing.

Knowing how to specifically tune into the Voice of Intuition not only helps to have accurate communication from spirit guides. You can also check in with your *intuitive feeling-place*. The guide's verbal message will also intuitively "feel right." This helps you to trust the meditation experience.

This easy-to-learn intuition access method will serve you well for the rest of your life. It truly leads to spiritual mastery.

As well as using your Voice of Intuition to easily interpret your dreams and meditation symbols—it is also a way to understand the meaning of the metaphors of life. In addition, you can ask your Voice of Intuition to decipher mysterious symptoms in your body. You can discover the hidden causes of pain and illness. Most illnesses have an underlying emotional cause. Do a meditation with a healing guide to find and then heal this memory.

The **"Intuition Location-Finder Exercise"** helps you discover specifically "where" you hear your Voice of Intuition. *(This spot is found either near the head area, on the surface of the head, or within the head.)* This exercise need only be done once. If you have trouble visualizing, it is beneficial to discover how your verbal intuition communicates with you. Your Voice of Intuition helps you to understand more about imagery seen in meditations.

The Intuition Location-Finder Exercise©

Set Up

1. Think about several intuitions you had in the past.
2. Select a <u>positive</u> one to use for the exercise.
3. Write down the details of the intuition you selected.

NOTE: *You did not have to realize that it was an intuition at the time you had it. When you think about it now, you are pretty sure that it was intuitive input.*

Examples:

- You somehow *knew* something good was going to happen, and it did.
- You had a good feeling about an action to take. You then followed the intuitive guidance, and it turned out to be a wise decision. For example, you heard about a workshop or training, signed up for it, and it turned out to be a life-changing experience.
- Perhaps you were intuitively led to the right person, place, or thing. Intuition may have directed you to a newspaper ad for the perfect job offer, apartment, car, etc. Or, a certain book seemed to jump off the shelf. You opened it randomly and found what you most needed to know.

You can also choose an intuition from the past that had an impact, such as:

*"When I met her, I just **knew** she was the woman I would marry."*

Or, "When I first saw him, my heart told me he is the perfect man for me."

The Intuition Location-Finder Exercise©

Part 1

Your Intuitive 'Feeling Right' Place

In this exercise, you will discover the location in your body where an intuition **feels right.** The specific intuitive feeling place is usually found somewhere between the throat and the gut. For many, it is in the upper chest area.

With some, the feeling is in one specific spot and stays there. For others, it moves. It starts in one place—then moves in an upward motion.

> *NOTE: If the feeling moved in a **downward direction**, it means you had a secondary feeling of fear **about** the intuition. If this happens, you chose an intuition that made you nervous or worried. Instead, choose a different, positive intuition for the exercise. Better yet, choose three different intuitions and go through the exercise with all three in turn.*

STEPS:

1. Sit in the appropriate posture for clearly receiving intuitions: Body upright, spine straight, shoulders back. Chin must be level.

2. **Close your eyes.** Pretend that you are back in the moment of time when you had the intuition. What was the exact statement that felt right?

    For example: This house (apartment) is the perfect one for me.

3. Hear that exact statement in your mind. Hear it repeated over and over. Notice that the intuited message gives you a "feeling of rightness" in your body.

4. Scan your body with your mind's eye. Find the exact spot where you feel this "feeling of rightness."

5. Hone in on the exact location where the "feeling of rightness" is strongest.

    Place the palm of your hand over that area. Does the feeling:

    - Stay in that one spot?
    - Intensify?
    - Move? *Gesture to indicate this movement.*

Note: An intuitive feeling can expand throughout the chest. It can move up. It can move up and then down the arms. But it does <u>not</u> usually move downward in the body. If you had a downward movement, you may have had a secondary feeling of fear, worry, concern or mistrust about the intuited message.

STOP HERE and record your findings. Then, move on to the next part of the exercise.

The Intuition Location-Finder Exercise©

Part 2

Your Intuitive Voice

You will now be identifying the exact spot where you **hear** your **Voice of Intuition.** Think of it as the place in your mind where intuitive thoughts pop-in. You may not hear an actual voice. It may seem more like a passing thought going through your mind.

The most common locations of the Voice of Intuition:

- From several inches to a foot or so outside of the head. This can be in any direction: From above, over to one side, near the back of the head, or out in front of you.

- OR: It may be on the surface of the head. There are several places it could be: At the temple, middle of the forehead, back of the head, or top of the head.

- It can sometimes be heard in, or just outside of one ear, or in both ears (stereo).

- Or, it is sometimes located within the brain. If there, it is often right in the middle, but can be any spot in one of the lobes.

PREPARATION:

- Use the same intuition example you chose at the start of this exercise.

- Hear that intuitive thought statement repeated over and over, just as you did in the previous exercise.

Have straight posture. Keep your chin level. As you listen to the intuitive statement, hone in on the exact spot where you hear the voice the strongest. This is like fine-tuning with a radio dial to get strong and clear reception from a broadcasting station.

Or, you can think of your eyes as tiny satellite dishes that are honing in on a signal.

If the voice is heard behind your peripheral vision, look at that spot with your mind's eye.

GOAL: You want to pinpoint the exact spot where you hear your voice of intuition. Scan by using your mind's eye. You want to find the <u>exact</u> spot where you hear it the strongest.

Begin scanning. You should find the location of your Voice of Intuition while doing ONE of the following three steps. You should explore all three to make certain.

1. **Do you hear intuition outside the head, in space?**
    - Start by scanning entirely around the outside of the head.
    - Keep hearing the intuitive statement as it is being repeated.

If the intuitive voice is found in space outside the head, its location may be inches away, or can be further out—up to a foot or more.

Notice: Is it a moving communication? That is, does it originate at one spot and then flow toward the head?

If you are certain you have found the location of the voice while exploring Step 1, you can skip ahead to Step 4.

2. **Do you hear intuition on the surface of the head?**

    Keep hearing the intuitive statement as it is repeated over and over.

    You will now be searching on the surface of the head.

    With your mind's eye explore the following locations:
    - the temples
    - middle of the forehead
    - at, or just inside one or both ears
    - at the back of head
    - at the top of head

    If you still have not found its location, explore further. Go to Step 3.

3. **Do you hear intuition inside your head?**

    Keep hearing the intuitive statement repeated over and over.

    Scan in the following areas:
    - behind the eyes
    - the inside of the forehead
    - Inside one or both ears
    - within the brain

4. **Touch your head, or gesture in space** to indicate the exact location where you hear your voice of intuition.

5. **Journaling:** Record the location of your Voice of Intution

NOTE: If at this point, you still have not yet found the location of your Voice of Intuition, it may be too subtle to enable you to pinpoint its source. **If so, turn up the volume**. Keep hearing the chosen intuitive statement repeatedly—each time louder. Recheck all locations in the steps above. Also, repeat the exercise with three different intuitions.

Part Three

CONCLUSIONS

Think about the intuited verbal statement and the good feeling *(feeling of rightness)* that you had in response to what you heard. What was it about the intuition that allowed you to trust it?

> *Most people report one or more of the following qualities about verbal intuition: It is gentle, benevolent, and yet authoritative. It is worth listening to. It has a calm certainty. It is like hearing advice from a friend you can trust.*

Journaling Your Discoveries

Record the specific locations of your Voice of Intuition and your Feeling Place of Intuition in your journal. It is helpful to make a line drawing of your body.

Put an X on the exact spots...

1. Where you felt intuition...(the place where it "feels right.")

2. Where you heard your Voice of Intuition...

    Remember: To hone in to your Voice of Intuition and hear it clearly, it is important to look directly at the spot where you heard it the strongest when you did this exercise.

Chapter Twelve

OVERCOMING YOUR FEARS

I have counseled many people who told me they were fearful of intuitive input. For some, to be intuitive made them too different from their friends. Some people have told me that they didn't like knowing things other people had no way to know. They couldn't understand the gift in this form of intuition until I explained it to them.

Still others didn't know how to understand what they were "receiving" (like the young boy in the movie *The Sixth Sense*). When they learned that they could use this to help others, it gave them a big sigh of relief.

A few were taught by religious leaders that they might invite in the devil if they saw spirits or worse, listened to them. Fear of the devil made them shut down their intuitive senses.

It is true that some people will not understand anything they cannot see. It is so good to have supportive friends of *like-mind*. They are out there. I have found and made many intuitive, spiritual friends by attending holistic fairs, going to metaphysical bookstores, attending classes on meditation, yoga, psychic development, and so on. I have led dream groups and meditation groups in my home for nearly thirty years. As a result I have made many wonderful friends that support my beliefs. There are spiritual support groups in your community. Seek them out. Or, start your own group.

Skepticism, or fear?

I believe in healthy skepticism. You should always measure any suggestions made in this or any other book against your own feelings. Doubt is ok. This feeling is an internal signal system. It is supposed to keep you from trusting blindly. But don't let doubt stop you cold. It will abate when your protective parts see that spiritual input actually does help you.

While doubt can be useful, fear is another matter, especially when it comes to spiritual guidance. When you call on a spirit guide and meet one, the resulting feelings will be that of trust, calmness, and/or lightness—not fear.

Fear can stop you from getting the spiritual assistance available to you. Fear is heavy. It draws your attention down into the lower part of your body. Spirit cannot get through to you if you are focused downward into your fear-body. When doing a meditation, never slump or look down. A hunched over posture prevents spirit guides from coming through your intuitional pathways.

Why would you fear working with a guide?

If you were taught as a child to fear God, you may perhaps feel uncomfortable with the notion that either God or the spirit liaisons of God will help you whenever you ask. You may have been taught that you are unworthy. That is nonsense. Spirit wants you to be the best you can be and will give you all the help you ask for. Because there is the spiritual rule of free will, though, you must ask for it.

Are you agnostic? You do not have to think in terms of spirit guides if that concept doesn't work for you. There is another way to think about guidance. Consider it in these terms: You may have realized in the past that you did not have all the answers. You may have said that you needed to "sleep on it" before making a decision. If so, can you now believe that you have an inner intelligence working on your behalf? Think about this…what is the source of that intelligence?

Is there perhaps a deeper part of you that is more-knowing than your conscious mind or ego? In the past you may have already listened to and trusted what you describe as your own *inner voice*. You may be familiar with your inner *feelings of rightness*. If so, then I encourage you to experiment with the shorter meditations in the last chapter of this book.

Perhaps you can become comfortable with the idea that you do have an *inner helper* that you can call on whenever you want or need to. Amend the suggested wording or phrases in the meditations. State that you want to communicate with your inner helper or inner intelligence. Be open-minded. You will get good results.

A few have told me that they were taught by their religious leaders that to tune into good spirits will invite in evil spirits. That is such an unfortunate belief system. So many have been helped tremendously by the legions of good spirits. They will come to the aid of humans who are often so much in need. Why limit yourself and be unaccepting of this help out of fear?

To be stuck in fear is to stay stuck in fear. That is not good for your body or mind. Fear can stop you from having a rich and full meditation experience. If you are fearful but want to try accessing a safe, positive spirit guide—I recommend that you ask to meet with your angel. An angel guide will feel safe.

You may be fearful that you cannot do the meditations well enough. If you are feeling fearful for any reason, it is wise to do the following exercise before doing any meditation to meet a guide. Ask your ego-mind to step aside and allow your intuitive-mind to lead you through this exercise.

Exercise

RELEASING FEAR

Worry, concerns, stress and fear can be released with this simple exercise

1. Fear is like a ball of energy that is stuck within a specific place in your body (or brain).

2. Think about your fear. Pinpoint the exact spot in your body where you feel it.

3. Pretend you have x-ray eyes and can look within.

4. Look into the area of your body that holds the feeling of fear. You will see it as a darkish color. Most often it is black, but can be any <u>opaque</u> or color such as red, orange, yellow, dirty grey, ugly green or muddy brown.

5. Ask Spirit for your clearing color. The color or colors that come to mind will be light and transparent. They may be misty.

6. Breathe the clearing color into the place where you hold the fear. Surround the fear color with your in-breath and gather it up. Breathe the fear color out forcibly and put it into a strongbox. Do several clearing breaths.

7. Close the lid of the box. Send it either to the middle of the earth or to the sun to be burned up.

8. Next, ask Spirit to surround you with Spirit-light. What color is this? Breathe the color of this light into the area that had held the fear.

Am I making this all up?

It's very common for the ego to question imagery seen in meditation. You may wonder "Am I making this all up?" If you are hearing this question go through your mind, ask your ego-mind to step aside and stay quiet during the meditation. Invite the ego-mind back in at the end to help you take action on the guidance provided.

When your eyes are closed and you begin to breathe slowly and deeply, your muscles automatically begin to relax. Within five minutes your brain waves change from beta (an eyes-open pattern) to an alpha brain-wave pattern. This state invites the intuitive part of your brain to accommodate Spirit participation.

When Spirit is invited, imagery comes that may surprise you. You may receive communication you would not have thought of. I liken the alpha state imagery to a dream, therefore I call these meditation journeys "wide-awake dreams."

How can you tell the difference between true Spirit guidance and interference from ego?

How can you know if you truly are getting spiritual guidance? How do you know if your subconscious or your ego is interfering by telling you what it thinks you want to hear?

First of all, guidance from Spirit 'feels right.' Spiritual truth feels like lightness in your body. You may feel tingles on your arms. It can bring tears of joy.

If it is negative-based, a message from your ego or subconscious will not feel right. It will feel heavier in your body. The feeling will sink.

A true spirit guide would never hurt you or have you hurt anyone else in any way. Options and suggestions can be made by guides, but not demanded.

For example: If you are in a dangerous, abusive relationship, you may get a spiritually-led message suggesting that you can <u>choose</u> to find a way out of it.

On the other hand, a protector guide or your Higher Self may shout at you to alert you if you are in immediate danger. In the instance above, if the abuser intended to kill, maim, or harm you, your intuition or a spirit guide may yell out "Leave NOW!"

A spirit guide would not fuel up your anger at another, be critical, or have you be judgmental. For instance, if someone hurt your feelings, a spirit guide would help you to find compassion, kindness, and forgiveness.

Spirit guides help you find the positive intention for the actions of others. If, for example, your mother-in-law criticized the way you handle your children, a spirit guide would help you to understand her positive intention. The guide may lead you to see that she is acting on her own beliefs, and help you understand that she has your children's best interest at heart. A spirit guide would teach you to find more positive ways to react and show you how to have a sense of humor.

A true spirit guide does not criticize you for your actions, but would gently advise you to do things in more positive ways. While communicating with a spirit guide, you should feel calm, serene, uplifted. The guidance received will *feel right* in your body.

The "Intuition Location-Finder Exercise" given in the previous chapter is designed to show you the difference between spiritually-led intuitive guidance and ego input—in minutes. If you feel fearful about inviting in a spirit guide, be sure to do the intuition exercise in the previous chapter and the exercise in this chapter to release fear before undertaking the meditations.

Chapter Thirteen

WHAT YOU NEED TO KNOW BEFORE DOING A MEDITATION

A meditation can take several forms

Many of the suggested meditations are short, usually taking only from five to ten minutes. (Although the first one in the last chapter is an in-depth teaching meditation and can take fifteen to twenty minutes.)

Each meditation is designed to enable you to have a visual journey to meet with a specific type of spirit guide. From that point on you will be interacting with the guide in some way. All meditations begin with suggested (guided) imagery and then at a certain point, allow Spirit to take over and create your experience. When that happens, the meditation becomes a *wide-awake dream.*

There are of course, many different types of meditation. Others you may have experienced or heard of may be somewhat dissimilar or totally different from the type in this Practical Guide.

For example, there is a type of meditation in which you sit quietly, pay attention to your breath, (or a mantra) and quiet the mind totally. The goal is to become closer to the Higher Power and to become more enlightened. For most people, however, it is difficult to sit quietly and think of absolutely nothing for twenty to thirty minutes. The average person's mind wants to fill itself with all sorts of thoughts. That can be distracting. It takes practice to get adept at meditating to quiet the mind totally. While this form of meditation is useful, it is not the kind I suggest in this Practical Guide.

Self-hypnosis is a deep form of meditation. It puts the brain into a theta brain wave pattern. Theta is what happens to your brain when you are just about to fall into deep sleep. In this type of meditation, you count yourself down into deeper and deeper levels of consciousness. Self-hypnosis is useful to instill affirmation statements. It can be used to reprogram the subconscious mind for self-improvement and change negative beliefs and behaviors. Theta brain wave patterns take about twenty minutes or more to accomplish. It can bring one to a deeply relaxed state and helps to invite deep, relaxed sleep. I prefer that my readers are alert and aware during a meditation so that they can interact with the experience and remember it. Therefore, self-hypnosis techniques self-hypnosis techniques are not included in this book.

The short meditations given in the last chapter are designed to put your brain into an alpha pattern within five minutes or less. In alpha state you stay awake and aware. You can interact with your guides, ask questions and receive quick guidance on any subject of your choosing. You can of course sit with a meditation a bit longer than the intended few minutes if it is interesting and is provides information that is useful to you.

More about brain wave patterns

There is a scientific component to meditation. According to Laura Silva of the Silva Manifestation Programs—when your eyes are open, your brain wave pattern is in "beta." 85% or more of what goes on in your brain happens through outer visual stimuli. For that reason, it is difficult or impossible for most people to meditate with their eyes open. That is why a meditation usually starts with the suggestion to close your eyes. When you do so, you are actually shifting the receptors in your brain.

Here is the simple form of entering meditation: When you close your eyes and begin to breathe slowly and deeply, your brain begins to settle into the "alpha" brain wave pattern. Biofeedback has shown that the muscles in your body begin to relax. When your brain is in alpha, it is the perfect brain-pattern for guided imagery meditation. That is why all the meditations begin by saying: "Close your eyes. Breathe deeply. Take at least three to four long, slow, deep breaths." When your brain is in alpha, you are still alert enough to participate in the imagery and interact with the guide.

About the steps in each Meditation

The rest of this chapter takes you through each step in a meditation, so that you will have a heads-up on what to expect.

Have an intention in mind

It's important to set an intention before beginning a meditation. Please write your intention(s) down on a piece of paper or in your journal. Writing them down is important because it tells all aspects of your psyche that you are serious about this endeavor and that you expect results.

Simple intentions:
- To meet your spirit guide, or Higher Self, or angel, or power animal.
- To have an interactive communication with a guide.

Profound intentions:
- Think of specific questions you want answered
- Ask for healing

Some of the meditations have longer pauses in which you can ask a question and receive an answer. In that case, you will want to have questions written down before starting the meditation. Your prepared question also sets an intention.

Good questions that provide quality answers can be found within the meditations in the last chapter

One of the meditations is designed for healing. A healing guide takes you on a journey into your body to find cause or reason for a body symptom. Therefore your intention should specifically be what you want to heal.

Releasing stress

Every meditation starts with an exercise to release stress. This is important to do before welcoming in a guide. It allows a lightening up of the body and mind. It helps to relax the muscles.

Different suggestions are made in the various meditations for how to do stress releasing. These include: Breathing in clearing colors (Spirit provides these) and breathing out the stress (which can be mucky or yucky colors). Or, putting stress in a dumpster or metal strongbox (rocks or boulders may drop into them), then having it hauled off. Or, forcibly breathing out and sending stress up to the sun or to the middle of the earth to be burned up.

Think "recycling." Sometimes you just need to get rid of junk for good. However, it may fit better for you to recycle your negative emotions into positive things. When you send stress into the earth, you can see it turned into fertilizer. Negative stuff put into a dumpster can have a label that says "Recycle Bin." When you do the releasing techniques, be creative.

Creating a safe space or envisioning a sacred place

Before having an interaction with a guide, you want to start from a safe and peaceful place. If a guide takes you on a journey out of the safe place, you always want to return to it at the end of that journey. If you find a troubled younger-self during the experience, you always want to take it to your safe place. That is where healing happens.

What is an appropriate safe place?

The place or landscape you experience in the journey will be based on where you feel safest in life, and what you believe a Spirit realm might look like. Perhaps you have had a safe, peaceful place in real life. Or you may have created one in a previous meditation.

When I have led groups to go to their safe, peaceful, sacred or healing place, many have seen either a wonderful meadow—perhaps filled with flowers, an open place surrounded by trees; a beautiful garden; a seashore, or a gentle waterfall. Others are taken into a sacred temple. Some have found themselves in a beautiful cave full of crystals.

Whatever it turns out to be for you, it will be a place or landscape that makes you feel totally safe and at peace. Some people have had a safe, fun place in their childhood which may come to mind, such as a backyard playhouse, swing, or sandbox. It's important that while envisioning this place and then entering it, your body feels light, free and your mind feels at peace.

The above suggestions are common places others have gone to in their meditations. But, don't have a pre-conceived idea about what it should be. Now that you have read the suggestions, let go of them. They are intended to help your creative mind know how to tailor the safe place to your exact needs. When entering the meditation, close your eyes and allow your imagination to create the right safe place for you.

Welcome in guiding spirits and/or power animals

All the meditations include meeting a guide. You will welcome in your guide after you are in your safe, peaceful or sacred place. Your intention will welcome in the appropriate guide(s).

Communication with your guide(s)

After you meet with the guide, you will tell it your intention. Remember the purpose of a meditation is to interact with your spirit guide(s). You can ask any question. You can ask for guidance. Your guide will communicate with you in one or more ways. It can converse telepathically–that is, you will hear it speak in your mind. The guide may also show you symbols or images. These can appear sequentially. Imagery can come in metaphor–which will be like watching a play or movie.

Much like a dream, everything you see in a meditation has meaning. As an example, every color means something personal to you. Two or more colors swirling together mean something more than each color would mean separately. If a color comes up in answer to a question, look into that color with your mind's eye and ask your intuition what it means to you. If at some point you only see black or darkness, ask your spirit guide to shine a light into the dark for you. Ask and it will be so. When light is brought in by spirit, you will be able to see what was hidden within the dark. The way light is provided can be symbolic such as a torch, a lantern, a flashlight. Or, it can be Spirit light streaming in from above.

Guides can be clever in the way they help you. I counseled a teenage girl who had felt sad much of the time. This bad feeling had gone on for several years. When I asked where she felt the sadness, she pointed to her chest. I asked her to look within the feeling and tell me what she could see in there. But, all she could see was blackness. Seeing only black or darkness is a common situation when looking into the place where one feels a negative feeling. But there is always something hidden within the dark and usually that is a younger self stuck in a bad memory.

To help her discover what was hidden within the dark, sad feeling I asked her to call on her guide. In response, a white wolf appeared. This animal felt protective to her and helped her feel safe. I asked the wolf to bring light into the darkness. The wolf cleverly produced a flashlight that he held in his teeth. This made the girl laugh. When the light spilled into the darkness, she could then see a classroom with everything in disarray. She peered further in and found a younger self sitting in a corner, downcast and sad. This younger self explained why she felt so sad. A very mean teacher had yelled at her in front of the class and she still felt bad about it. Even though this had happened two years before, she had never released the sadness, so this sensitive younger self had gotten stuck in that emotion. Once the distressed younger self was found, we could bring her out into the light and take her to the safe place. Once there, her guide could help the younger self understand that the teacher was incorrect in what he did. She didn't have to stay forever locked into that classroom. She could move on from that memory.

The gift

Every meditation ends with a guide giving you a gift. It commemorates the experience and is a reminder for the future. During the meditation, take it into your heart and allow the energy of it to flow through your body.

Other things you can do with this gift:

- Find a picture of the symbol (or create one) and hang it up.
- Make a vision board and put this symbol in the center.
- You may be led to a store where you find the exact object.
- You may already own this object.
- In whatever form this symbol shows up in your life, put it where you can see it everyday.

Grounding yourself

During a meditation, your consciousness has traveled, perhaps far. This is not typically an out-of-body experience, but it is considered to be mind-travel. After the meditation is completed, consciously return to the present. **Always** bring the life-force energy into your body. Allow it to flow into the top of your head and flow down into your body, arms and hands, legs and feet. Make sure you are back to the present and fully in your body before driving a car. Drink plenty of water after a meditation journey.

Journaling

Always record everything you remember as soon as you open your eyes. Meditation experiences are much like dreams and quickly fade.

Chapter Fourteen

PREPARATION FOR MEDITATION

Spirit is light. Your body is of course–denser. However, your body will begin to feel lighter when tuning into Spirit energy.

It's to your advantage to meet and greet your spirit guides. Once you do that, you can call on them, communicate with them and intuitively interact with them at any time that you wish. The next chapter has several meditations that will help you meet different types of guides. Suggestions are provided for how to interact with each of them.

**Have an open mind.
Allow Spirit to provide the imagery.**

Meditations can be perceived in several different ways. For example: the information can come in a straightforward manner – that is you can have a conversation with a guide and hear the answers telepathically in your mind.

But sometimes, your guide will show you things—perhaps a memory, or a vision in the form of a metaphor. Or, it may show you colors, objects or symbols. In other words, a meditation can be much like a dream. Therefore if you see these kinds of things in a meditation, they are symbolic and have meaning. If you are watching something that seems like a movie or a play (and it is not a memory)—then it is a metaphor (that is—a story that has deeper meaning, such as in the tale of the Ugly Duckling.) If you are unsure what the symbols and metaphors mean, ask your guide to explain. Look directly at the spot where you hear your Voice of Intuition for clear and accurate meaning.

If you have not yet done the "Intuition Location-Finder Exercise," do it now. Find it in Chapter Eleven.

Different ways to be led through a meditation

1. Memorize the steps. This can work well for the shorter meditations.

    Ask a part of you to be the observer. Instruct this part to give the steps to you in sequence as your intuitive mind goes through the meditation.

2. Make an audio recording of the steps. Provide generous pauses in-between each step to allow you to process the suggestions made.

3. Have a friend or partner read the steps to you.

Make sure the other person reads them slowly, with generous pauses in-between each to allow a full experience. You can have predetermined hand and finger signals. You can hold up your hand if the facilitator goes too fast. And, crook a finger downwards to indicate when you are ready to move on.

4. Listen to my audio recordings. All meditations and exercises in this book are available as downloads on my website. There is a special private link to get this package at a 66% discount…

    See Link #2 on page 128 – "RESOURCES."

Before you begin a meditation

Have paper and pen ready. Meditations are much like dreams and can quickly fade. You will want to record your experiences when you open your eyes. Use a journal or record the experiences in a file on your computer.

Write down your intention

This helps your conscious mind and all aspects in your subconscious to have the same, specified focus. Your intention also tells Spirit to provide the exact guide and guidance you need. Think about what you want to have happen during the meditation. Each meditation in the next chapter does have an intention to meet a particular type of guide. However, you may also have a personal second intention such as:

- I request the answer to (*insert your question*):_____
- Or, I am seeking healing for*:* ___*(state the issue or problem.)*___

You certainly can ask previously unplanned questions as you go through the meditation. Feel free to ask your guide any questions that come to mind.

Get comfortable

Sit in a comfortable chair that allows your body to relax. The correct posture for intuition is to sit with spine straight, chin level, eyes level or looking slightly up behind closed lids.

Be in a positive frame of mind

With enthusiasm say to yourself: Yes! Yes! Yes! That should bring feelings upward in your body. Also, imagine the best thing that ever happened to you. Visualize and feel how it felt at the time. These suggestions will greatly help to get you into the right intuitive mindset before starting a meditation. ☙

Chapter Fifteen

MEDITATIONS

Meet Specific Guides

Each of the meditations in this chapter will bring a particular guide to your conscious awareness. The meditations are designed to acquaint you with spirit guides and as well as the realm of Spirit in a comfortable way.

You don't have to do meditations in sequence. You don't have to do all of them. Pick and choose the meditations that feel right to you. The same one can be done several times over a period of time.

"Power Animal Meditation" can help you to meet the same power animal each time you need its particular power. Or, the meditation can be done many times, to meet different power animals for different needs.

"Meeting a Guide" can be done each time you start a project or have a specific need.

"Higher Self Meditation" Is beneficial to do whenever you need to communicate with the higher aspect of your soul.

You may have only one specific guide or power animal that shows up in a meditation. However, if you have already met several guides and power animals, more than one can appear in the *same* meditation. If you know that you have many guides, you can ask for any of those who want to be with you to come along on that particular journey. The guides that want to support your intention are the guides that will appear.

Most of the following meditations in this chapter normally take from five to fifteen minutes. You can probably do the shortest meditations without a facilitator.

The first meditation in this chapter, however, may take twenty minutes or longer because it includes important details that teach you how to have a rich and full meditation experience. It will help you understand how to do the rest of the meditations in a thorough manner. It would be useful to have someone read the steps to you for this first one.

Don't rush through the meditations. Any one of them can be made longer or shorter. Take all the time you need with each step. Allow Spirit and your guide(s) to have free rein to provide surprises.

The steps in each meditation are guidelines. They do not have to be strictly adhered to. It is important to be open-minded. Allow and accept your experiences. You may begin with my suggestions, and then feel free to go in any direction. During a meditation experience, be sure to ask the questions that may pop into your mind.

Meditation #1

MEET AN IMPORTANT SPIRIT GUIDE

NOTE: This is an in-depth meditation. It teaches you to slow down and breathe deeply—which relaxes the muscles. It provides detailed instructions for releasing stress. Do this releasing technique in the same way in every meditation before you ask to meet the specific guide suggested.

Use this first meditation as a model for how to prepare your mind and body for every meditation experience. The others in this chapter make brief suggestions that pre-suppose you know how to flesh out the experience.

State your intention. "I am going to meet the spirit guide that I most need to know about right now."

1. Close your eyes.
2. Take a deep, slow breath.
3. Now, imagine a dumpster out in front of you.
   Breathe out all stress and worries and send them into the dumpster.
4. Ask Spirit, "What is my clearing/releasing color?
   Take in a deep, slow clearing breath of this color.
5. Imagine that this clearing breath goes slowly through your body. Send it into the sore spots in your body. See the clearing color surround and gather up all stress, and worries held in those sore spots.
6. As you breathe out, you may see the out breath as dark, mucky or murky colors. Send these into the dumpster. You may envision symbolic objects–such as rocks or boulders pouring out of you and going into the dumpster.

7. Take three more, deep, slow clearing color breaths. Imagine them going into any remaining sore/tight or dark spots within your body.

8. On each out-breath, put whatever comes out with it into the dumpster.

9. Check within your body with your mind's eye. If you still see dark spots, do a few more clearing breaths.

10. Imagine that a huge truck comes up, attaches itself to the dumpster and drives it off to the dump (or the recycle center).

11. Notice that your body feels lighter, calmer.

12. Connect with your heart center. Think about someone or something that you dearly love. Feel the feelings of loving energy.

13. Imagine that you are in a safe, peaceful place. This may be a place you have been in another meditation, a place you know from real life, or it can be something brand new to you.

14. Breathe slowly. Relax. Allow a bit of time to feel the peacefulness and serenity of this place to touch your skin.

    With each gentle breath, imagine peaceful energy flowing into your body. Visualize each breath as a calming color and watch and feel it as it gently swirls through your body. Feel this peaceful energy soothing every cell within you. Your body feels lighter and at peace.

15. Explore your peaceful, safe place.
    Become familiar with it.
    - What do you see?
    - What do you hear?
    - Are there any fragrances?

    It is almost time to meet your spirit guide. Intend to see your guide in solid form—as if it were a being. Although, it is perfectly fine if you see the guide as brilliant color(s). Or, as an accumulation of energy in the air.

16. Ask for the guide that is important to meet right now.
    It is a guide that wants to connect with you.
    When the guide appears, greet it. If you don't <u>see</u> the guide, then *how* do you perceive it? Perhaps as a feeling?

17. Begin to interact by asking the questions in Step 18. As you ask each question **pay attention to how the guide communicates with you.**

    - You may hear it speak as if in verbal conversation. Or, you may hear it in your mind like a telepathic message.

    - Or the guide may not speak at all but instead show you things. It may take you on an experiential journey.

    - Or you may just get feelings. If so, tune into them. Remember that the feelings have a voice and can give you answers.

18. Ask the guide these questions:
    a. "Why are you important to me?"
    b. "What do you do for me?
    c. "How can I best utilize your talents, skills and power?"
    d. "What do you most need from me?"

    Do you have any other questions? If so, go ahead and ask them now.

19. Hold out your hands, palms up. The guide gives you a gift. This gift commemorates this meeting and is a symbol of what the guide's power is for you. Bring this gift up to your chest and then let it go into your heart. Feel its energy flow through your body.

20. Thank the guide for everything it helped you to learn.

21. You are ready to return your focus to the present.
    Ground yourself. Feel your feet firmly on the floor. Feel the life-force energy flowing into you.

Feel this tingly energy flow in from the top of your head, down into your arms and hands, legs and feet. Become fully present.

Remembering everything you experienced…gently open your eyes. Write down everything you remember.

Follow-up steps

As you record your experience, be sure to include all details:

- Describe your peaceful place.
- If you saw the guide, what did it look like?

    If you didn't see it how did you perceive it?
- How did the guide answer your questions?

How did the guide communicate?

- > Visually *(Did it show you things?)*
- > Auditory *(Did the guide talk to you?)*
- > Kinesthetically *(Did you feel what the guide wanted you to know? What did the feelings say to you?)*

- What else did you see and/or experience?
- What was the gift?

The gift you received is important. It commemorates this meeting and represents what the guide does for you. The gift may have been something the guide said. Or it may have been a symbolic object. If so, this may be something you already have. Or, you may be intuitively led to a store where you find it. Someone may give you this item. Or, it may be something you can create (like a clay sculpture, painting, drawing, collage).

Put this object or art piece where you will see it every day.

You may not have understood the meaning of some of the imagery shown to you. Perhaps you did not know the meaning of the gift. This is the point when it is useful to know the location of your Voice of Intuition. Use the specific, directed eye-movement that you learned in the "Intuition Location-Finder Exercise."

Go over the list of symbols and metaphors that you saw in the meditation—one at a time. Ask intuition what each symbol means. Next to each symbol, record the meaning given by your Voice of Intuition.

You can use your intuition directly within the meditation to decipher the meaning of its symbols and metaphors as you experience the journey. During the meditation, pause and ask: "What does that mean to me?" Your Voice of Intuition will give the answer immediately.

NOTE: In the meditation above, explanations and suggestions were given in detail. By doing this first meditation you will begin to understand how a guide can interact with you and how you perceive its communication. It will help you to become familiar with how you receive and process intuited information.

RESOURCE: Get the audio recording of this meditation. It is the longest meditation in this chapter. Therefore, it would be much easier for you to go through the steps by listening to my voice as I lead you through them. This meditation is included in the companion package to this book. The downloadable recording includes all the meditations and exercises.
See LINK #2 on page 128 - "RESOURCES"

Meditation #2

CALL ON A SPIRIT GUIDE FOR A PARTICULAR NEED OR PROJECT

State your Intention: "I call on a spirit guide for_____ *(name the need or project).*

Close your eyes.

1. Take at least 4 deep, slow, clearing breaths.

2. Have each breath gather up stress and throw it into a dumpster. You can also send it to the sun to be burned up.

3. Connect with your heart center by thinking about someone or something you dearly love.

4. Imagine you are in a safe, peaceful, place or scene.

5. State your intention. Ask for the guide that can help you with your need or project:_____

6. Greet the guide. Feel its calming energy.

7. State your intention. Ask the guide for help with your need or project:_____

8. Communicate with your guide:

    a. Ask: How can I best utilize your talents, skills and/or power for my project/need?"

    b. Ask the guide: "What do you most need from me?"

    c. Do you have any other questions? If so, ask them now.

9. Hold your hands out, palms up. Receive a gift from this guide.

10. Take this gift and bring it into your heart. Allow the energy of it to flow throughout your entire body.

11. Bring your energy fully back into the present.

12. Gently open your eyes. Record everything you experienced.

NOTE: Each time you do this meditation, you can change your intention to meet a different guide.

For example, if you are writing, you can ask to meet a writing guide. If you want to learn something new, ask for a guide that is knowledgeable about that subject.

Meditation #3

MEET YOUR GUARDIAN ANGEL

Intention: Ask to meet your guardian angel.

1. Close your eyes.
2. Take at least 4 deep, slow, clearing breaths.
3. See a dumpster. As you breathe out, ask to release all stress.
4. Connect with your heart center. Think about someone or something that you dearly love. Feel the feelings of loving energy.
5. Imagine you are in an angelic scene that feels sacred and peaceful.
6. Ask for the angel that has been guarding you. Do you see your angel? Or, sense that it is with you? Perhaps you feel its loving touch.
7. Your angel embraces you. Feel its loving energy flow into you.
8. Ask: "What do you want me to know about you?"
9. Hold out your hands, palms up and receive a gift from your angel. Bring the gift into your heart.
10. Return your focus to the present. Feel the life-force energy flowing into you, from the top of your head, down into your arms and hands, legs and feet.
11. Gently open your eyes. Feel the loving presence of the angel still with you. Record everything you experienced.

Meditation #4

MEET YOUR POWER ANIMAL

Intention: Ask to meet with a power animal

1. Close your eyes.
2. Take at least 4 deep, slow, clearing breaths.
3. With each out-breath release stress and put it in a dumpster. Or, send it to the sun to be burned up.
4. Connect with your heart center. Think about someone or something that you dearly love. Feel loving energy flow through you.
5. Imagine you are in a safe, peaceful place in nature.
6. Ask for a power animal that is guiding you or ask for one that can guide you for a special need.
7. When you see the animal, ask it what it symbolizes for you. (I.e. Bear might mean strength. Owl might mean wisdom.)
8. Ask: "What do you need from me in this partnership?"
9. Hold your hands out and receive a gift from it.
10. Return to the present. Bring your energy fully back into your body.
11. Gently open your eyes. Record everything you experienced.

NOTE: You may have more than one power animal. You can do this meditation several times to meet more of your animals.

Meditation #5

MERGE WITH YOUR POWER ANIMAL TO FULLY FEEL ITS POWER

This is an expanded version of Meditation #4

Intention: Ask for a power animal that wants to merge with you so you can FEEL its power. You can call on the same power animal from the previous meditation. Or you can ask for the animal you need right now.

1. Close your eyes.

2. Take at least 4 deep, slow, clearing breaths.

3. With each out-breath, release all stress. Put it in a dumpster. Or, send it to the sun to be burned up.

4. Imagine you are in a safe, peaceful place in nature.

5. Ask for a power animal you previously met. OR ask for one that you most need right now.

6. If the animal is new to you, ask it what it symbolizes for you.

7. Allow your mind to fully merge with the animal. Imagine that you are fully within its mind and body. Become the animal. See out of its eyes.

8. FEEL the animal's power. Feel its 'medicine.' The animal may go on a journey while you are within it. This will give you the experience of *shape-shifting*. It will give you a better idea of how to utilize the animal's energy, guidance, wisdom and more.

9. Step out of the animal.

10. Invite the animal to step into you and merge with you.

11. FEEL the animal's energy within your body and mind. This action will translate / transmute the animal's power into your human being-ness. This will give you the feeling tone of how best to make the animal's power your own.

12. Ask the animal and your intuition what the next step should be:
    a. Should the animal stay within your body?
    b. Or, is it best that the animal step back out of your body and be alongside you? If so, the animal's energy/power can stay within.

13. It's time to return to the present. Keep the energy of the animal within you as you bring your life-force energy fully back into your body.

14. Gently open your eyes. Record everything you experienced.

NOTE: You can do one of both power animal meditations to communicate with the same power animal or meet new ones.

Meditation #6

MEET YOUR HIGHER SELF

Set the intention: Ask to meet with your Higher Self.

Secondary intentions:
- You can use this meditation to manifest your desired goal.
- Higher Self holds your soul blueprint. You can ask for your soul blueprint to be rekindled and remembered by the body's cells. This is useful for body issues (such as an overweight) and body distress (such as pain/trauma from accident.)

1. Close your eyes.

2. Take at least 4 deep, slow, clearing breaths.

3. With each out breath, send stress and/or emotional baggage with into a dumpster. Or send it to the sun to be burned up.

4. Connect with your heart center. Think about someone or something that you dearly love. Feel loving energy flow through you.

5. Imagine that you are in a safe and peaceful landscape. This is a starting point. From here you will travel to meet with Higher Self.

6. Ask to be taken to the sacred realm, or dimension of Higher Self.

    a. Do you believe the Higher Self is within? If so, start this exploration by looking in your heart. If the sacred realm is not there, then scan around in your body.

    b. Do you perceive this realm as above? If so, then imagine a way to get there, that is, some means to get "up" to it.

    You may see: stairs, or an elevator or escalator
    or a mountain with an easy path up to the top;
    or, you may float or spiral upward

7. When you arrive there, ask Higher Self to appear as a being, as an image in solid form.

8. Greet this being. Thank it for all it does for you. If you have something you want help with—state it now.

9. Ask Higher Self, "What do I need to know right now?

10. Ask your Higher Self, "What do you need from me?"

11. Ask HS to make its Voice of Intuition louder and stronger so you can hear it clearly.

12. Hold out your hand and receive a gift.
    Hold it to your chest and allow it to go within your heart.

13. Thank your Higher Self for this meeting.

14. It's time to leave this realm and return to your safe place.
    Go back the same way you came.

15. Return your focus to the present. Fully feel the life-force energy flowing into you through the top of your head. Feel it flow through your body, into your arms and hands, legs and feet.

16. Gently open your eyes. Record everything you experienced.

NOTE: You can do this meditation often. It is especially good to do when you have an important question or request, want or need.

Meditation #7

MEET A MONEY GUIDE

In my dream and meditation groups we have called on guides for just about everything you can imagine. Sometimes people don't think of asking directly for money. Asking for abundance is good, as long as you welcome money as a part of it. Almost everyone can use more money. Why not ask Spirit to help you manifest it? You can ask for a personal money guide or seek a financial assistant guide.

Part One

Set your intention. Ask to meet with a money guide. Or you can ask for a financial assistant, money manager, or abundance guide.

1. Close your eyes.
2. Take at least 4 deep, slow, clearing breaths.
3. Release stress and emotional baggage with each out-breath. Send all negative stuff into the dumpster, or send it to the sun to be burned up.
4. Connect with your heart center by thinking of a person, place, pet or thing that you dearly love. Feel the energy of love flowing through you.
5. Imagine you are in a place of abundance and that there are symbols of wealth all around you. (Pots of gold, gold bars, money trees, treasure chests, or whatever comes to mind.)
6. Ask your intuition to help you find the special spot where you can meet with your money guide.

7. Ask for your money guide to come meet with you. When it comes into view, greet this guide with appreciation.

8. Ask: "What specific kind of guide are you?" *Money? Success? Financial assistant? Abundance?*

9. Ask: What can I do to have more money?

Pause the meditation here and record your experiences and everything you have learned so far. After you have done this, you can go back to your money guide and continue on with Part Two, which is designed to help you discover a limiting belief or block you may have about money.

Option: Or, return at later time to work with your limiting beliefs and blocks. If you decide to stop at this point, be sure to bring the life-force energy fully back into your body.

MEET WITH A MONEY GUIDE

Part Two

Transforming a Block or Limiting Belief about Money

In Part Two of this meditation, you can ask a money guide to help you discover what blocks you may have to accepting more money. You can ask if you have negative beliefs about money. When you discover a block you can ask your guide for assistance in overcoming it. When you find a limiting belief about money, you can ask the guide to help you transform it into a positive belief. It may be a "fact" that you don't have enough money. But facts can be thought of as negative beliefs.

Good questions to explore in Part Two of the Money Guide Meditation:

- What is a limiting belief I have about money?
- What block do I have about accepting money into my life?
- What do I need to do to make more money?
- What is a fear I have about money?
- What can I do about the financial stress I feel?
- What stops me from having money, (or success).
- Was I programmed by family to have negative feelings about money?

When you do Part Two of this meditation, ask only one question each time, and follow it through as suggested in the steps.

NOTE: If you are continuing the meditation from Part One, then you can start where you left off. If you are doing this on another day, be sure to go through the deep-breathing and clearing steps first.

Set intention: Choose only one question to ask your Money Guide.

1. Once again, imagine that you are in your abundance landscape. Ask to meet again with the same money guide.

1. Ask just one of your questions: (For example: "What is a limiting belief (or block) I have about money?"
   Hear or sense the answer.

2. With your mind's-eye look within. Find the place in your body where you hold that belief (or block). See it as a dark place or an object stuck within. Ask the money guide to remove it from you.

   If you find a negative memory, ask the guide to help you rescue your younger self from that scene. Take it to your safe *place.*

3. Ask the guide: What is a new positive belief (or image) to replace that negative one?

4. Ask the guide for a symbol to represent the new belief. Take this symbol and bring it into your heart. Allow the energy of it to flow throughout your entire body. See this symbol in every cell of your body.

5. Thank your money guide for this meeting. Ask it to be ever-present and guiding you in daily life.

6. Return to the present. Feel the life-force energy flowing into you from the top of your head, down into your arms and hands, into your legs and feet.

7. Gently open your eyes. Record everything you experienced.

Recommendation: Do this meditation often. People usually have anywhere from three, to up to twenty-five or more limiting or negative beliefs about money. You can find and work with a different issue each time.

There can be several different types of fears about money, such as fear of failure, fear of success, fear of others asking you for money, fear of being too good for friends or family. Ask your money guide to help you ferret out your fears.

Fears, worries, concerns and stress about money can get stuck in your subconscious and prevent you from having what you want. Every time you say "I can't afford that." Or, "I don't have enough money to pay my bills," you reinforce this as **truth** in your subconscious. Think of this as self-fulfilling prophecy. The subconscious believes what you say to yourself and will give you what you seem to be affirming for. The subconscious hears *"I don't have enough money,"* as an affirmation and translates that to make sure that you never have enough. This is your subconscious working for you—against you.

Use these money meditations to change your statements. For example "I do want that and ask my Higher Self to help me get it." And, "I always welcome in the money I need to pay my bills—on time."

Meditation #9

ASK FOR A HEALING GUIDE

We can all go through times of poor health. Some health issues are minor such as a bad cold, flu or cough. But even though minor, they can sometimes linger for weeks or run for a month or more.

Would you like to have a way to shortcut that time? Do this meditation when you first start to feel symptoms. Also, program a dream that same night and ask to be healed.

You can also do this meditation to transform emotional distress or ease pain.

NOTE: If you are having mysterious symptoms or pain, there could be a serious problem. You should consult a doctor. This healing meditation then can be utilized after the medical tests and diagnosis. In cases of chronic poor health and dire illness, this meditation can be useful as a healing energy companion to the doctor's advice and recommendations.

State your intention: I ask to meet with my healing guide. I want help and healing for _____.

1. Close your eyes.

2. Take 4 deep, slow clearing breaths. As you breathe out, imagine that all stress, worries and fears are released from your body and go into the dumpster; or are sent to the sun to be burned up.

3. Connect with your heart center by visioning a person, place, pet or thing that you dearly love. Feel the loving energy flow through you.

4. Imagine that you are in a **healing** place that is safe and serene. Allow the vision of your healing place to create itself. Be within this space. Look all around. What do you see? Are there any sounds? Fragrances?

5. There is a special spot in this place where you will meet your healing guide. Look around. Find the special spot. *Suggestions: A bench? A small temple? A pyramid?*

6. Ask for your healing guide to appear.

7. If you don't see your guide right away, don't try to force it.
   Enjoy the healing place for a few more moments.
   Breathe in the calm, serene energy.

8. Keep asking: "I ask for my healing guide to come and be with me."

9. When you in some way, *know* that the healing guide is with you, make this request:
   "Please help me heal this_____."
   *(Name the problem,
   or indicate the part of your body with the symptom).*

10. Watch, listen and feel what your guide does to help you heal:

    a. The healing guide may chant over you; or play a musical instrument.

    b. The guide may give you its healing touch.

    c. The guide will provide your unique healing color(s).

    - Tune into the distressed area. Breathe the healing color(s) into the dark spot in your body.

    - Breathe out the darkness.

    - Continue to breathe in the healing colors.

    - Do seven to ten of these healing breaths.

    - Your out-breath will begin to look like your healing color. The darkness within will fade, then become cleared. Your out-breath will then be the same color as the in-breath.

11. If you can be accepting of the answers, ask the guide:
    "What is the emotional cause of this illness (or pain.) "
    "Is there a bad memory related to this illness?"

12. Ask the guide, "What can I do to heal?

13. Hold out your hand and receive a gift.
    This is symbolic of the healing energy you received.

14. Thank your healing guide for this meeting.

15. Return your focus to the present.
    Feel the life-force energy flowing into you, from the top of
    your head, down into your arms and hands, legs and feet.

16. Gently open your eyes and record everything that you experienced.

17. Program a dream tonight. Ask your healing guide:
    "Please help me heal in my dream state."

NOTE: Get a bonus healing meditation that is not in this chapter. The audio recording package available as a companion to this book includes "A SHAMANIC HEALING JOURNEY." This bonus meditation has many guided imagery healing techniques that are not included in this chapter. **Go to Resource page 128. Follow Link #2.**

Meditation #10

MEET WITH YOUR SUCCESSFUL FUTURE SELF

Your future self certainly can be a *helper guide* for you. In this meditation, you first meet with a manifesting guide and then ask it to take you into a probable successful future. On your success time-line, you meet the future self who has become what you want to be. Your future self then can tell you how he or she was able to achieve the goal you seek. Steps to success are given.

Success can be anything from financial abundance, physical health, or weight loss, to being in a good relationship with a partner, boss, child or parent. Any goal you seek can be used for this meditation.

Set this intention: I want to meet my manifesting guide. This guide will take me to my future self who has become what I want to be.

1. Close your eyes.

2. Take at least 4 deep, slow, clearing breaths.
   Send all stress and worries into a dumpster.

3. Connect with your heart center. Think about a person, pet, place or thing that you dearly love. Feel this loving energy flow through you. Your body feels light and at peace.

4. Imagine you are in a place that embodies success; a place that feels like the energy of success and has symbols of success all around you.

5. Ask for your manifestation guide.

6. State your intention/goal: Tell the guide: "I want to meet the future self who has become what I want to be.

7. The guide shows you a path. It is filled with bright light.
   This is the path of your successful future. What does the path look like?

8. Walk along the path for a bit.
   You are walking a time-line.
   Now you can begin to see your future self in the distance.
   Where in time (on the line) is your future self? Six months from now?
   A year down the road?

9. As you approach your future self, notice:
   What is your future self's posture?
   Clothing style?
   Confidence level?
   What color or colors do you see surrounding future self?

10. Merge into your future self. Look out of his/her eyes.
    FEEL how it feels to have what you desire.
    Feel the energy of being what you want to be.

11. Step back out of your successful future self. But, retain the
    good feeling of already having what you want.

12. Ask your future self to step into and merge with you.
    FEEL how it feels to be this self.
    What are you saying to yourself about having met your goal?

13. Your future self steps back out,
    however the feeling of his or her success stays within you.
    ASK your future self: "What do you most need from me so that I can become you?"

    You can ask other questions, such as:

    a. What is the first step I need to take to manifest my goal?

    b. What are next steps I need to take?

    c. What one thing has made the most difference in going from who I am now to becoming you?

14. Hold your hands out and receive a gift from your future self.
    Place it in your heart. Feel it's energy flow through your body.

15. Your manifestation guide now takes you go back to your starting point on the path.

16. Turn and face your successful future self. See that your future self has grown so big, so bright and beautiful that you can clearly see him or her from this present moment point on the path.

- You can see threads of glowing and sparkling energy emanating from the future self

- This energy begins coming toward you

- Feel it surrounding your body.

- Feel the energy flowing into you.

- You are connected and are now being drawn in the direction of success by the threads of energy.

- Bask for a few moments in these powerful feelings.

18. Thank the manifesting guide for its help. Ask it to stay on task with you and remind you of the next step to take.

19. Return your focus to your body.
Feel the life-force energy flowing into you, from the top of your head, down into your arms and hands, legs and feet.

20. Gently open your eyes. Record everything you experienced.

Do a 30-day success program

Continue to meet with your manifestation guide and work with this future self once a day every day for 30 days. Also, program your dreams every night for 30 nights and ask to achieve this same goal. This double-whammy can help you accomplish what you desire because it reprograms the subconscious mind to give you what you want.

Meditation #11

MEET WITH A DECEASED LOVED ONE

Intention: Ask your guide to bring a dearly departed loved one for a visit. Or, if that's not possible, ask to be taken to where he or she is now. You can also do this meditation to hold and cuddle the spirit of a deceased pet.

1. Close your eyes.
2. Take 3 to 4 deep relaxing breaths.
3. Connect with your heart center. Think of the loved one and how much love you feel.
4. Imagine you are in a comforting, safe, serene place or landscape. Feel the peacefulness wash over you.
5. Ask for a guide or power animal that can help you meet with a dearly departed loved one. Say the name of the person you wish to see.
6. Ask if the deceased soul is free to visit with you in this place.
7. If not, ask the guide or power animal if it's appropriate to go visit the person—wherever she or he may be.
8. If the guide tells you that it is appropriate at this time to meet with your loved one, do what the guide tells you to do to prepare. If the loved one cannot be brought to you at this time, you may have to follow the guide to another *location*, where your loved one will be waiting for you.
9. Relax and send welcoming and loving feelings from your heart out to the memory of your loved one. Keep sending this love until the person you seek is brought to you or you are brought to where he or she is.
10. In the afterlife, a loved one who has gone to the Light is usually free to travel. He or she will look younger, healthy, and vibrant.

11. Communication with the loved one is possible. Say what you most want to say. Open your intuitive ears for what the loved one wants to tell you.

12. If your loved one has not yet gone to the Light and you sense that the soul is stuck, ask your guide what you can do to help.

13. Hug your loved one. Promise to be open to future visits. This can be in dreams or in waking life. Say a fond farewell for now. Let your loved one go.

14. Thank your guide for this opportunity.

15. Fully return to the present. Bring life-force energy into your body starting at the top of your head. Let if flow into you.

16. Gently open your eyes. You may feel a bit teary-eyed. Allow the feelings to flow through you.

ABOUT ME

Nationwide, I am recognized as a dream expert, with over thirty years experience in dream research.

In 1985, I created an innovative dream interpretation method called the "Dream Decipher Process" that has helped thousands of people understand the meaning of their dreams.

From my years of experience in working with dreams, shamanic journeys, meditations, and working with spirit guides, I have developed 5 to 10 minute, time-saving processes that give people a way to get spiritual guidance, on demand. These processes are taught in this Practical Guide.

My Private Session Specialty: I specialize in recurring dreams, nightmares, and all types of bad dreams and facilitate interpretations of any type of dream. You can do a session with me through Skype on the internet, or by phone. If you want to discover the meaning of your dream, contact me for an appointment at this email address: Tianna@DreamDecipher.com

See testimonials about my work on the EFT/Meridian Tapping Website:
www.TappingInternational.com – Practitioner search: Tianna Galgano

Website: www.TiannaGalgano.com
Contact email: Tianna@DreamDecipher.com

Follow me on my Facebook Fanpage – great hints and tips
Facebook.com/Tianna.Galgano.Dream.Coach

RESOURCE PAGES

Tianna Galgano is an experienced public speaker and workshop presenter. She has done presentations at NLP conferences from 1986 to present.

Now available for speaking engagements and workshop presentations in your area. Also available for radio/Internet interviews, or as a guest speaker on your hosted webinar.

AUDIO RECORDINGS - MEDITATIONS

Link #1 - Your FREE GIFT

Includes two meditations: "Meet a Spirit Guide" (Chapter 2) • "Meet a Power Animal" (Chapter 6).   Get the downloads here:

www.tiannagalgano.com/2-free

Link #2 - Special Discount Offer – MP3 Audio Package

INCLUDES all meditations in the last chapter, plus three exercises: "Intuition Location-Finder" • "How You Visualize Imagery" • "Releasing Fear"

Use this private LINK to get this entire package at a 66% savings. Plus, ORDER NOW and get a **bonus** meditation: "A Shamanic Healing Journey," included in the package.

www.tiannagalgano.com/audio-meditation-pack

DVD

DREAM WORKSHOP – Learn how to interpret your dreams. Two hour video instruction INCLUDES: "Dream Decipher Interpretation Process" • "Intuition Location-Finder Exercise" • "Discover the Meaning of Your Colors Exercise" • A meditation to get an answer to a burning question.

Available at: www.TiannaGalgano.com/store

OTHER BOOKS by Tianna

DECIPHER YOUR DREAMS, *Decipher Your Life*
SHAMANIC DREAMING, *Heal Yourself & Help Others in Your Dreams*

INTUITION TRAINING

AUDIO RECORDING - "Intuition Location-Finder Exercise"

Do you need further help in discovering the locations of your Intuition?

Listen to an audio recording while Tianna leads you through all the steps!

This exercise is included in the companion package to this book. This downloadable recording contains all exercises and meditations.

LINK #2. **www.tiannagalgano.com/audio-meditation-pack**

Use this private LINK to get this entire package at a 66% savings.

ADDITIONAL INTUITION DEVELOPMENT TOOLS

Would you like to expand your intuitive abilities, enhance your intuitive voice, and learn more about how to tune into and trust your intuition?

My book **Decipher Your Dreams, Decipher Your Life** will teach you how to develop and hone your intuitive senses. This book has a comprehensive chapter devoted to intuition.

Available at: **www.amazon.com; www.bookdepository.com; www.barnesandnoble.com** or **www.tiannagalgano.com/**

Also available in physical bookstores in Sedona, AZ, including: The Peace Place, Crystal Magic and Sedona Rouge Spa.

Made in the USA
San Bernardino, CA
11 October 2017